# BEYOND
# FETCH

# BEYOND FETCH

## FUN, INTERACTIVE ACTIVITIES FOR YOU AND YOUR DOG

## D. CAROLINE COILE, PH.D.

HOWELL
BOOK
HOUSE

**Library of Congress Cataloging-in-Publication Data:**
Coile, D. Caroline.
  Beyond fetch: fun, interactive activities for you and your dog/D. Caroline Coile.
    p. cm.
Includes index.
  ISBN 0-7645-1767-8 (alk. paper)
1. Games for dogs. 2. Dogs. I. Title.
SF427.45C65 2003
636.7'0887—dc21
                        2003001062

Manufactured in United States

10  9  8  7  6  5  4  3  2  1

Book design by Marie Kristine Parial-Leonardo
Cover design by José Almaguer
Illustrations by Kristin Doney

*Give your dog a lifetime of adventure,*
*and your dog will give you the adventure of a lifetime.*

# Contents

# Introduction

## YOU'RE INVITED . . .

You're invited to a game. You're invited to run, hide and play ball. You're invited to release your inhibitions and revisit your childhood. You're invited to laugh. You're invited on an adventure. Your dog is inviting you.

Why did you get a dog? Chances are it wasn't to experience the thrill of midnight walks in the rain, master the art of wood filling, or refine your carpet cleaning skills. You probably got a dog because you wanted a friend. But let's face it: You could have taken the easy way out by choosing almost any other pet. But you chose a dog because no other friend is as much fun as a dog.

Dogs love to play. It's part of their heritage. Most dog jobs are simply refined play skills. In fact, one theory of dog evolution is that dogs are wolves with arrested development. They retain their juvenile attributes, including the urge to play, long into adulthood. But the dog's urge to work and play can create problems for modern dog owners, who can't always hustle up sheep to herd for their Border Collie or organize a wolf hunt for their Borzoi. Unemployed dogs can be frustrated dogs, and they tend to seek new careers in the home demolition field. Appropriate play can redirect these dogs' energies into something both of you can enjoy a lot more than home destruction and home repair.

Most dog owners do play with their dogs. The most common game, fetch, is a good game—but it's not the best game for every dog. Some dogs see little reason to bring something back that you've just thrown away. Even for diehard retrievers, variety adds an element of surprise and adventure. Our goal here is to go beyond fetch, to map out new canine adventures, to go where no dog games have gone before.

Not every game is right for every dog. Some dogs are neither physically nor temperamentally suited for some games. And, like everything that deals with dogs, controversy exists over what dogs should play at all. You've probably heard all these warnings:

- Don't play keep-away games—your dog will learn he can run away.
- Don't play wrestling games—your dog will learn he can fight you.
- Don't play tug games—your dog will learn he can dominate you.
- Don't play chasing games—you will awaken your dog's prey instincts.
- Don't play barking games—your dog will learn to bark.
- Don't play treasure hunt games—your dog will learn to search your belongings.
- Don't play digging games—your dog will learn to dig.
- Don't play tag games—your dog will learn to chase people.
- Don't play jumping games—your dog will learn to jump the fence.
- Don't play tunnel games—your dog will learn to squeeze out of the yard.
- Don't play laser light games—your dog will become obsessive compulsive.
- Don't play games when your dog wants to—your dog will think he's in charge.

And the list goes on . . .

Each caveat has some merit. Dogs with aggressive tendencies shouldn't play wrestling games. Dogs with obsessive-compulsive tendencies shouldn't play laser light games. Dogs who want to run your house shouldn't get to dictate when playtime begins.

Every dog is different. *Some* dogs shouldn't play *some* games. Some dogs have no interest in some games. And some dogs become overly obsessed with some games. While appropriate warnings are listed with the various games, ultimately you are the best judge of whether that game is right for your dog.

I have left out several types of games. Games that encourage dogs to run down and attack people should not be entered into casually. While sports such as Schutzhund and French Ring Sport feature dogs having fun corralling "fugitives," that aspect is only a small part of what these dogs are trained to do. Attack training without absolute control creates dangerous dogs.

Games that involve killing captive animals, game hunting or fighting other animals are also omitted for humane reasons.

I've also left out most games that are thinly veiled obedience lessons or tricks. While some dogs love to learn tricks, other dogs find them about as fun as doing multiplication tables. School is fun, but recess is more fun!

Some activities require your dog to already know how to do something before you start. These prerequirements are listed along with each activity under "Abilities." Some require you to train your dog to do—or not do—something. Check out the Training Resources above for general training instructions.

## Training Resources

Burch, M. and Bailey, J., *How Dogs Learn*, John Wiley & Sons, 1999.

Reid, P., *Excel-Erated Learning: Explaining in Plain English How Dogs Learn and How Best to Teach Them*, James and Kenneth, 1996.

Tillman, P., *Clicking With Your Dog: Step-By-Step in Pictures*, Sunshine Books, 2001.

Karen Pryor's Clicker Training: www.clickertraining.com

Dr. P's Training and Behavior Page: www.uwsp.edu/psych/dog/dog.htm

No dog is expected to do everything here, but there should be something here for every dog. Check out The Best Mind Games for activities you and your dog can share indoors. See how you can exercise your dog without leaving the yard in The Best Backyard Athletics. Invite some human and canine friends over to play The Best Party Games. Head out to sample The Best Canine Events in your community. Hit the road to experience The Best Doggy Vacations. Hit the trail to share The Best Outdoor Adventures. Join others in showing off in The Best Organized Sports. Be creative and make some of The Best Dog Toys. And take some quiet time to bond while experiencing The Best Ways to Relax with your dog.

Dogs love to play. It's part of why we love dogs. So let's play!

# Chapter 1

# The Best Mind Games

What's there to do on a rainy day? How can you entertain a dog who can't handle strenuous physical activity? What can you do with your dog when you're too ill to take him out to play? Plenty of opportunities for entertainment await indoors. The games in this section can provide whole minutes of entertainment.

A well-rounded dog is not just a jock, he's also a scholar. By challenging your dog's intellect you can entertain, educate and even exhaust him. If you have a gifted dog who loves to learn, you can have plenty of fun teaching all kinds of tricks and games. If you have a chow hound, you can make him work for his supper. If you have an explorer, you can encourage him to search for treasures.

While some games may require a little learning, the object is not to learn tricks but to play games. The difference between a trick and a game is that unlike most tricks, no two instances of a game are ever the same. Of course, some dogs make sure they never perform a trick the same way twice, either.

1

# THE GAMES

## TREASURE HUNT
### SNIFFING OUT THE GOODS
**Abilities:** None

Is your dog good at sniffing out trouble? How about a game that lets him sniff out what you want him to? Start by letting your dog watch you hide a treat. Begin with a simple hiding place, such as under a chair. Then say "find it!" and let him go find the treat right away. Of course he gets to eat what he finds. Practice this until he knows what the game is about (this shouldn't take long). But that's too easy.

Next hide the treat under a blanket or behind some furniture without letting him watch exactly where you put it (although he should be close enough to see generally where you're hiding it). You might show him the food first, so you have his attention. Then have him watch you from behind a baby gate or other barrier so he can't grab the treat as soon as you put it down. Let him loose and say "find it!" Now he has to search for it with his nose.

You may need to encourage him, perhaps guiding him closer to the area where the treat is hidden. If that doesn't work, switch to a smellier type of food and try again. You may even have to lay a scent trail to the food by dragging it there—but before you resort to dragging greasy fried chicken over your furniture you may wish to move the game outdoors. In fact, save any really smelly foods for outdoor trials. Most people don't want liver-scented sofa cushions. Not only are they unsettling to dinner guests, but the lingering odor could entice your dog to search for treats inside the cushions one day when you're not home.

## TOTAL RECALL
### A MEMORY-BUILDING GAME
**Abilities:** None

If you've already taught your dog to use his nose to find hidden goodies, he may think he's pulling a fast one on you with this game. In fact, you're going to try to prevent him from sniffing out the treats by using nonsmelly food and sealing it in plastic containers. That won't prevent him from smelling it if he really tries, but it may make him more likely to use his memory instead of his nose.

Let your dog watch you hide a treat or toy, perhaps under a chair or in a drawer. Make a big deal out of placing it in its hiding place. Then take him to another room and wait with him for 30 seconds before returning to the room and saying "remember where?" He should be able to remember and go right to it as soon as you let him loose. If he doesn't, start again from the beginning, but wait only a few seconds and build up to a longer time, or use a more tempting (and thus more memorable!) treat.

Gradually make him wait longer and longer, and even add distractions while waiting. For example, you can practice some tricks or play catch for 10 minutes before letting him go for the treat. Too easy? Let him watch you hide several treats all over the house. How many can he find without searching? Can you build his memory with practice? Can he do it in the dark?

## SHELL GAME
### A SLEIGHT-OF-HAND CHALLENGE
**Abilities:** None

You don't have to go to the big city to play a shell game. The rules are simple: Place one piece of round dog food under one of three opaque plastic cups. Place these cups on a slick surface so you can easily slide them along with the piece of dog food under one. Unlike the big-city version, you won't need shills to attract customers and your dog won't be laying any bets. Nor will you be pulling any funny stuff; the piece of food will really be under one of the cups at the end of the game!

Start with only one cup. Show your dog the piece of food and let her watch you put it under a cup. Tell her "keep your eyes on the prize!" and encourage her to nose the cup. When she does, give her the food.

Once she realizes that she gets the treat when she noses the cup, add a second cup to the equation. Let her watch you slide them both around and switch locations. If you want her to use her nose, always place the treat under the same cup so only that cup has the treat's strong scent. If you want her to rely more on her eyes, place the treat under either cup.

If she chooses the correct cup, lift it up and give her the treat. If she points to the wrong cup, lift it up so she can see nothing is under it and then start the game again. Once she's doing it well with two cups, add a third cup. The hard part is adding a third hand!

As her skills improve, work on your own skills at shuffling and sleight of hand. Bet you can't beat her!

Don't have any cups? Just use your two hands and let your dog nose the one with the treat.

## AMAZING!
### MAKE A DOGGY MAZE
**Abilities:** None

Have a lot of time on your hands? Then a doggy maze is for you! You can start your maze with just a few pieces of stiff cardboard or lightweight panels that are taller than your dog. The hard part is making them stand upright. (If you were outside, you could drive tent stakes or poles into the ground. But most people don't like doing that inside to their floors.)

Try using PVC pipes with suction cups or braces on the bottom. For small and medium dogs, a bunch of toilet plungers can serve as uprights. With either, attach the cardboard sections to them with large alligator clips.

Start by making a mini-maze, perhaps just a straight line with an entrance and an exit a few feet away. No, it's not because your dog is stupid, it's so he can learn that getting to the exit gets him a treat. Place him at the entrance and shut the "door" behind him. Go to the exit and call him; you may have to come and get him at first. Once he is running to the exit, add a turn.

Next, add a T-shape so he has to make a decision; going one way leads to a dead end, while going the other leads to the exit and treats. Continue to make more panels and add more T's. Let him figure it out for himself. He can investigate the entire maze, finding which turns lead to dead ends and which to the eventual exit. This is part of the learning process, and unless he gets discouraged he shouldn't need too many hints from you. Of course, a little encouragement never hurts.

Once your dog understands the concept, you can start making very complicated mazes. Be sure you can disassemble the whole thing so your friends won't think you're weird when they visit.

Your dog may try to sniff his way out. If you want to encourage him to use his nose to find the exit, you can drag a scent trail along the correct path each time. But you may have to change the location of the maze often, because too many lingering or crossing scents could prove to be confusing. If you want him to use his memory from one trial to the next, you'll want to make sure your scent, as well as his, is evenly distributed on the floor and the panels.

## SOFT-SHOE SHUFFLE
### *BUILDING BAD HABITS*
**Abilities:** None

Do you have trouble walking across the room because your shoes have a canine attachment? Puppies love to chase our shoelaces and—even though the experts tell us we are teaching our dogs to chase our feet or eat our shoes, and we're setting ourselves up to be tripped big-time—it's fun to sit in a chair and shuffle our feet around while the pup goes crazy attacking them. If you have a death wish, it can also be fun to shuffle and run. Just be careful you don't fall or kick your dog's teeth out in the excitement.

## LOVE SEAT
### *A SILLY LOVE GAME*
**Abilities:** None

Here's a sickeningly sweet game that a couple of my dogs love. It's an indoor game for dogs who like to cuddle right next to you. You have to allow dogs on your furniture to play. It usually works best if your dog is already in a playful mood or interacting with you. Then you suddenly say, "I think I'll . . . sitoverhere!" and run over to a big easy chair and plop down in it, leaving a space to one side and holding out one arm beside you as if your arm were around your best buddy.

Dogs who are inclined to play will rush over and leap in the empty space in the chair. But you jump up after only a second and say, "or maybe I'll . . . sitoverhere!" and run to another chair and do the same thing. The game continues as you go from chair to chair to sofa to bed, sometimes tricking the dog by going back where you just came from. Make sure your chairs can't topple over backwards.

This game is so insipid that I would suggest not playing it around company. If you are a large person and have a small dog, be very careful before plopping into the chair—your dog may have beaten you there!

## BABY STEPS
### HOW TO ANNOY YOUR DOG, STEP-BY-STEP
**Abilities:** None

Here's another silly diversion that lasts only a few seconds. You can play it indoors, and it can also be a fun way to liven up a droopy dog any time. The premise is simple: You are going to "help" your dog walk by moving her front feet for her.

Ask your dog if she thinks it's time for a "walking lesson" and then reach over and gently grasp each front leg just below the elbow. Now move the right leg forward, then the left leg, so she is stepping along but moved by you. Some dogs turn into statues and other dogs are too complacent to make it fun. Most dogs will put up with this for about five steps before they buck like a pony and jump away from you to go on a running binge. Just watch your face so you don't get a bloody nose from a bucking dog!

## LASER TAG
### GO TOWARD THE LIGHT
**Abilities:** Desire to chase

For this game you need a dark area, a flashlight (or better, a laser light pointer) and a frisky dog. The rules are simple: Encourage your dog to chase the light as it travels around the floor. Some dogs merely yawn; others find this game irresistible. Take care that you don't shine the light in your dog's eyes and that you don't run him into a fence or tree or wall as he chases the light around.

This is a game that requires a serious caution, despite its innocuous appearance. For most dogs, chasing a point of light is a fun diversion that they forget as soon as the light disappears. For a few dogs, chasing the light becomes a compulsion. These dogs live to find the laser light, staring at floors and walls as though they expect the light to suddenly appear. In extreme cases they even stop eating or interacting with their family. If your dog displays any signs of becoming addicted to the laser light, stop playing immediately. Jack Russell Terriers and Bull Terriers seem especially susceptible to this problem.

## OVERACHIEVER RETRIEVER
### A FETCH GAME FOR BIG MOUTHS
**Abilities:** Retrieve

Here's a stupid pet trick for smart dogs who can't stand to give up one ball to pick up the next. They consider it a challenge to see how many balls they can stuff into their mouths at once. You can help out by handing the balls to your dog one by one and helping adjust them in her mouth, and then by encouraging her to pick them up by herself.

One big warning about this game: Never be tempted to use any ball she could inhale or swallow. Even tennis balls may be too small for some dogs. I'm not sure what the record is, but be sure to take a picture of your dog's personal best.

## HIDE AND SEEK
### YOU HIDE, HE SEEKS
**Abilities:** Stay while you are out of sight; come

Dogs have as much fun playing hide and seek as kids do—and they're better at it! The only thing they're not good at is counting to 100 before they start seeking. That means you either have to place your dog on a stay and then call him, or wait until he's in another room before you call. Either way, it's part of his sneaky plan to make you give away your hiding place.

Start hiding in easy places: behind doors, in closets or under tables. Then move to harder places: the bathtub, under the bed or in a cabinet. Any children playing this game should be cautioned about choosing only safe hiding places. Try to resist the temptation to jump out and say "boo!" when your dog finds you. OK, only do it if your dog thinks it's funny. You can boost enthusiasm by handing out a treat when you're discovered.

As your dog hones his skills, you can move outdoors and start hiding all over the place. Taking turns with a friend who can hold your dog while you hide enables you to really challenge him. You can go farther away, climb trees and if you're especially daring, hide in shallow water. Not only is this a fun game by itself, but it is also a good foundation for more involved games of trailing and of search and rescue. For added fun, play in the dark!

## Mutt 'n' Button
### A TREAT-FINDING GAME
**Abilities:** None

Remember the child's game of "button, button, who's got the button?" A group of people sit in a circle with the detective (your dog) in the middle. He can either be placed on a stay or held by one person there. The people in the circle pass a dog treat behind their backs from one person to the other, until it reaches the person who is selected to keep holding it. Then everybody brings their hands out in front of them, closed as though they were holding the treat. The dog is released (if you're feeling particularly festive you can say "mutt 'n' button") and allowed to walk around until he finds the treat in the right hand. Once he nudges the hand, the treat is his.

## On the Hunt
### MAKE DINNER AN ADVENTURE
**Abilities:** None

Does your dog wolf down his food as soon as you set the bowl down? Dogs have it too easy. Their wild ancestors had to hunt for food, but domestic dogs only hunt as far as their food bowls. Your dog will benefit, both mentally and physically, from the challenge of searching for his dinner if you hide his food bowl in a different place every day.

You can use some of his dinner to make a food trail leading to the bowl. Use dry food, unless you want a slimy floor. You can also hide his food in several small bowls in different hiding places. This is especially good for slowing down fast eaters. Even dogs who tend to have picky appetites will often eat when they've hunted down their meal.

## CROSS-EYED TREAT TRICK
### *BALANCING A DIET*
**Abilities:** Catch a treat

Here's a trick that most dogs enjoy. You've seen it before: A dog balances a dog biscuit or treat on his nose, then, when given the go-ahead, pops it up in the air and catches it. True, some dogs have noses better suited for holding treats than do others, but it's worth a try.

It's easier to teach this to dogs who already know how to catch a treat in the air. Here's how to teach that: Show your dog a tasty treat that won't knock his teeth out when he catches it. Toss it toward him so it moves in an arc that would land just behind his nose. Chances are it will bounce off his nose and onto the ground, and he will go pick it up. Beat him to it and grab it before he can (unless he's food aggressive, in which case you should pick another game). Try again. Eventually he will figure out that the only way to beat you to the treat is to grab it before it hits the ground. When he does so, let him eat it and be sure to act like you're in awe of his talent.

To teach him to catch the treat off his own nose, place the treat on his nose near the tip (but not on the tip—that tickles!). Say "hold it . . . " while gently steadying his head for a second or two, then say "catch it!" as you let go. As before, the treat will probably plop onto the ground and he'll go to grab it. As before, you will beat him to it. He's been down this road before, so it won't take too long for him to figure out he's got to nab it before you can get your paws on it, and to do that he has to grab it as it falls. Repeat—and repeat and repeat—until your dog learns to twist his head so the treat falls into his mouth. You can help by placing the treat so it is almost falling off one side of his muzzle.

Once he can catch it—and this may take awhile—work on having him balance it before catching by saying "hold it . . . " and steadying his head for a few seconds before saying "catch it!" If he tries to catch it before you say the word, stop him or grab the treat from him and start over. But have pity—don't make him balance it for too long!

## RISE AND SHINE
### *YOUR OWN CANINE ALARM CLOCK*
**Abilities:** Wake up people

Chances are your dog is the only one in the family who loves to wake up early. And chances are he makes it his mission to wake you up. Why should you hog all that good attention? Teach your dog to wake up everybody else in your family when you tell him "rise and shine!" Make the rounds of everyone's bed and encourage him to jump on them, pull back the covers and kiss them good morning.

If he needs more encouragement, just hide dog biscuits in the sleepyheads' beds every morning. Go with him and urge him to seek out the treats, or give him a treat when he kisses the sleeping person or otherwise wakes them up. Don't try this with a cranky riser, though.

Sure, this may be a little more work at first, but eventually you can just tell your dog "rise and shine!" and drift blissfully back to sleep as he awakens the rest of the family. Just think of how grateful they will be.

## SING FOR YOUR SUPPER
### *A HOWLING GOOD TIME*
**Abilities:** A tendency to howl or vocalize

Do you wish you had a singing partner? Some dogs love to talk and sing, especially when you join in. You can teach your dog to sing with you by finding out what makes her vocalize, then adding a command just before she begins. So if a siren sets her off and you hear a siren approaching, chime in with "call for help!" just before she begins to howl. You can even join in. Give her a treat afterward and she'll soon be calling 9-1-1 just to get a siren coming down the road. With only a few repetitions, she should start singing as soon as she hears your prompt.

## RED LIGHT, GREEN LIGHT
### A GAME OF STOP AND GO
**Abilities:** Sit, go wild

This is a variation of the child's game red light–green light that doubles as a training game. The object of the game is for your dog to go wild when you say "green light!" and to sit as fast as possible when you say "red light!"

First teach your dog to sit. The easiest way to do this is to hold a treat above and slightly behind her eyes, so she has to bend her knees and reach up for the treat. As soon as she does, give it to her. If she tends to just walk backwards, try placing her rear toward a wall or corner next time. Gradually require her to get closer to a sitting position before rewarding her, until she is finally sitting for a reward.

Once she knows how to sit, encourage her to go crazy and jump all around. You can even cue this on command: "green light!" Say "green light" and start running around and doing whatever makes your dog go dogwild, praising her for joining in.

Now combine the two by saying "red light!, Sit!" while she's being manic. Reward her as soon as she sits for a second, then say "green light!" and let her go wild again. Repeat, asking that she remain sitting a little longer and longer before you say "green light!"

This is a fun game because it combines activity, fast reactions, self-control and treats. It's also useful when you need your dog to calm down quickly. Sometimes the best way to teach your dog to control wild behavior (or any behavior that's not always appreciated) is to teach her to perform that behavior on cue. That way, she learns there's a time and place for everything.

## FIDO DO-SI-DO
### DANCES WITH DOGS
**Abilities:** Heel, learn some other moves

Admit it. Sometimes, when it's just you, your dog and the radio you've closed the curtains and had a canine cotillion. You've done a cha-cha-cha with your Chihuahua, mamboed with your Malamute or waltzed with your Whippet. And it was fun.

You can dance with your dog like you did when you were a kid, encouraging him to put his paws on your shoulders and do a slow dance (assuming he has no back problems this could aggravate). Or you can do a modern dance and jump all around while he just stands there and stares at you in amazement. But the most fun is when both of you learn a few dance steps and dance together.

If your dog already knows how to heel or how to do some simple tricks, you can have him heel in a circle next to you, take a couple of steps forward and then backward, weave between your legs as you step, bow to you or pirouette. You can choose music and choreograph routines to make the most of your dog's two left feet (and two right ones). Use lots of treats; remember, this is for fun!

Check out www.canine-freestyle.org/articles.html for some helpful hints on training your dog to do dance steps. One more thing: If your friends and family start worrying about your sanity, you can point out that doggy dancing is now a real sport called musical freestyle (see page 148).

## PUP PSYCHIC
### *IS YOUR DOG A MIND READER?*
**Abilities:** Three tricks of any kind

Does your dog seem to know what you're going to do before you do it? Does she possess mysterious psychic powers? Perhaps it's time to whip out your crystal ball, don a long robe, fire up the incense and test your dog's ESP. The problem is that while your dog may know what you're thinking, how will you, a mere mortal, know what she's thinking?

Here's one way. Teach your dog three different tricks in response to three different visual or voice signals. Before you give each command say "ready?" so your dog will know a command is coming. So you might say "ready? . . . sit" or "ready? . . . speak" or "ready . . . go outside"—depending on your three trick choices.

Write the name of one command (say, "sit") on five index cards; another command ("speak," for example) on another five cards; the third command ("go outside") on five more cards; and nothing on a final five cards. Shuffle the cards and pick the top one. Your job is to telepathically tell your dog to do the trick on the card you picked.

Say "ready?" but don't follow with a command. Instead for one minute visualize yourself giving the command for, and your dog performing, the trick on the card you've picked. For example, if the top card says "sit," imagine yourself telling your dog to sit and she, in turn, sitting. If your dog doesn't do anything after that minute, tell her the command so she can earn a treat. Repeat this for all the cards. For the blank cards, think of your favorite song or of anything but a dog trick.

How often does your dog perform the correct trick? Do you think she can read your mind?

## ROVER RECIPES
### *COOKING UP CANINE CUISINE*
**Abilities:** Eat

Another rainy day, and what's there to do? Dogs like to do anything that involves food—and that includes preparing it, as long as they get to lick the spoon! Let your dog share in the excitement of making some simple doggy delights. But don't just slop some dog food in a bowl; make something special.

For a hot summer treat, make some "pupsicles" by filling ice cube trays, plastic bowls or paper cups with yogurt and mixing in anything that sounds good, including diced carrots or apples, chicken or peanut butter. Freeze and serve!

For a country flavor, make liver bread using corn bread mix right out of the box, but substituting pureed beef, pork or chicken liver for milk. Cook for a slightly shorter time than usual, then cut, give some to your dog and freeze the leftovers.

Want to prepare something more gourmet? The Internet has many doggy recipes available (see the box on page 14). You can also improvise by preparing almost any human recipe and adding liver. Be sure to let your dog know this is something special you're making just for her. Make a big deal out of showing her all the ingredients and letting her sample them as you put them in the mix. Let her watch you mix the ingredients and let her taste it as

## Recipe Sources

Dog Biscuit Recipes: www.geocities.com/NapaValley/2049/doggie.htm

Dog Treat Recipes: www.twodogpress.com/twodogpress/dogfood.html

Doggie Connection's Recipes: www.doggieconnection.com/recipe/

Dogs Are Gods: dogsaregods.hypermart.net/recipe.htm

Favorite Dog Treat Recipes: home.gwi.net/~seadog/treats.html

Fuzzy Face's Recipes: www.fuzzyfaces.com/lrecipe2.html

Pooch Food: www.liferesearchuniversal.com/poochfood.html

The Poop Pantry: www.thepoop.com/pooppantry/default.asp

you go along, assuring her excitedly that this is for her. You might even let her wear an apron to really make her feel involved!

## BOWSER BUFFET

### A TASTE-TESTING TEMPTATION
**Abilities:** Eat

Here's a lazy day game your dog will eat right up. It may not seem like dazzling entertainment to you, but for your dog, what could be better than your undivided attention and a choice of dog treats?

This is a game that lets your dog tell you what his favorite foods are. You'll need to gather several different brands of dog treats. Make them as equal in size as possible. The most obvious way to find your dog's preferences is to line up all the treats and see which ones he eats first. But some gluttons just go down the line and eat whatever they come across first, even if it's a dead bug. Especially if it's a dead bug. Some other dogs tend to always eat from right to left or left to right. So you have to shuffle the order in which you line up the treats.

If you're really interested in learning your dog's preferences, try pitting one treat directly against another. Place one treat each in separate bowls and let your dog sniff each one, but don't let him eat them yet. A good way to do this is to lay a screen over the two bowls. Then remove the screen and let him choose just one. Keep repeating until you have a clear winner. Then test two other treats against each other. Finally, test all the winners from each round against each other in a play-off countdown until you have a champion!

No longer will you face hours of bewilderment in the dog treat aisle. Besides, you'll have so many boxes of treats you collected for the taste tests you won't need to buy any more for a very long time.

## SICK AS A DOG

### GAMES YOU CAN PLAY FROM YOUR OWN BED
**Abilities:** None

So you're sick in bed and your dog wants to play. Ugh! This is one time you wish you had a nice calm dog who just liked to cuddle. But instead you have a manic dog intent on pawing you and woofing at you and doing everything she can to make you get up and lock her out of your room. You might as well give in and play. It won't take much energy and what else did you have planned?

You can play all sorts of games while you lie there on the verge of consciousness. Put your dog through her paces and have her do every trick she knows in exchange for treats. Throat too sore to give commands? Play "paws off," in which your dog jumps on the bed and you grab at her paws, making her do a jig to avoid you, until she goes crazy and jumps off the bed and runs in circles before getting brave enough to jump back up.

Too exhausted for that much activity? Throw a ball down the hallway and let your dog fetch. Extra points if it bounces off the wall a few times or makes it up or down a stairway. You lose points for every lamp you break. Too weak to throw a ball? Strap a tug-of-war toy on your wrist and see if your dog can haul you out of bed.

Too sick for any of this? Cover your head with the sheets and just hope your dog will give up before she digs you out. Hide a bone under the bedspread and let her hunt for it. Turn on an electric toothbrush and let your dog go crazy digging for it under the covers. Or try 52-bone pickup. That's when you take a handful of dog bone treats and throw them up in the air so they land everywhere, giving you a chance to snooze while your dog scarfs them down. Make sure the bones are very small or you'll find yourself cleaning up after 52-bone throw up—and that's definitely not going to help you feel better.

And get well soon; your dog is waiting!

## Chapter 2

# The Best Backyard Athletics

Some dogs can get a workout running around an apartment. Some dogs need half a state. But most dogs can work up a sweat (if dogs *could* work up a sweat) in their own backyards. The advantage of playing in your backyard is that your dog won't run away when you're winning. The disadvantage is that your neighbors will be firmly convinced that you've been out in the sun too long. Privacy fencing is a wonderful investment.

Because backyard activities can be physically demanding for your dog, like any aspiring athlete, your dog should get a physical before he gets physical. Also like any athlete, your dog should warm up and cool down before and after exercising. Many dogs have far greater willpower than physical power, and it's tempting to both of you to overdo it when you discover a new fun activity. You're the member of the team who is supposed to have good sense; as your dog's coach, you're the one who should end every game before your dog tires. Tired dogs are more prone to injury, and a single injury will undo every bit of good all your conditioning may have accomplished. It's much easier to prevent an

17

injury than to fix one. Even if overdoing an activity doesn't cause physical injuries, your dog could come to associate the activity with being tired or having sore muscles, and may not be as keen to play in the future. As coach, you need to be aware of when your dog's muscles are sore, and perhaps order a massage (page 187) instead of a workout.

# THE GAMES

## GET IT!

### *THE ORIGINAL GAME OF FETCH*
**Abilities:** Desire to carry items

Before we go beyond fetch, how about a little fetch? The best time to start teaching a dog to fetch is when he's a pup, but it's never too late to try. Start by finding out what your dog likes to carry. Balls and squeaky toys are traditional favorites, but many pups prefer soft, scrunchy items. Feathers and furs are always attention-getters. Soft paint rollers (ones that have never been used) make ideal retrieving items for larger puppies. Even a section of hose can make a great retrieving item.

One of the secrets to culturing an avid retriever is to only bring out the retrieving items when it's time to play fetch. Keep them put away between games so your dog knows he only has this rare opportunity to play with them. It makes the game more fun for him than it would be if they were the same items he tripped over all day long.

Next there's the matter of throwing the item enticingly. Some dogs prefer rolling items, whereas others prefer bouncing ones. Sometimes letting an object ricochet off a wall helps increase interest. Sometimes throwing it only a short distance helps and sometimes throwing it a long distance helps. In other words, experiment. If he's still not racing to retrieve, you may wish to try racing him to the item a few times.

Once he chases it and picks it up, encourage him to bring it back by calling to him excitedly, perhaps even running in the opposite direction. Of course, your pup usually wants you to chase him instead, and while that can be a fun game, it can promote a lifelong habit of playing keep-away rather than fetch.

A good way to teach young pups to bring items back is to sit in the middle of a hallway. Throw the item to one end and send the puppy after it. Entice him back to you and as soon as he relinquishes the toy throw another toy a short way down the opposite end of the hall. Keep this up and he will naturally begin to run out, run back enthusiastically, give up the toy and get ready for the next toss. The toss of the second toy is the dog's reward, and sometimes the dog will drop the first item before he gets all the way back to you in his impatience to get to the second one. Make sure you don't throw the second item before he's delivered the first one. Encourage him to pick up the item he dropped and next time try a shorter distance. But don't get caught up in demanding he bring it precisely to you. Fun is more important that perfection!

Gradually increase the distance. You may have to move outside once your pup outgrows your hallway. Don't overdo the game; you don't want him to associate retrieving with getting tired. You always want to leave him wanting more.

## ONE IN A MILLION
### SCENT DISCRIMINATION
**Abilities:** Fetch

Have you ever wished your dog could find your car keys? You can teach your dog to find items you've handled and bring them to you. It's a fun game that might come in handy one day.

Some dogs are naturals at this. A good way to start is by picking up a stick while you're on a walk and making a big deal over how this is a "special" stick (see page 167 to review stick safety precautions). Show it to your dog as you run your hands over it, marveling at the wonders of the special stick while rubbing your scent on it. You may even wish to breathe on it. Practice having him retrieve it a few times. Then find some similar-looking sticks and let him see you throw the special stick among them. Tell him something like "find mine!" or "special stick!" He should be able to bring back the right stick with no problem. Praise him mightily for bringing back the special stick.

Next, throw the special stick into the pile of sticks so your dog can see only approximately where it lands. Now he has to use his nose to find the right one. Don't hurry him; if he's interested he will probably find the right one eventually. If he's way off course you can lead him over to the general area and give him some hints.

This game is a lot of fun on walks because it doesn't take any preparation, but there's one very big word of caution. Large piles of sticks can harbor poisonous snakes or other dangerous animals. Don't send your dog into such places if there is any chance of him encountering an unwelcoming homesteader.

Some dogs need more help to understand what you want. You can train them using several identical items of any sort, all but one of which are wired to a piece of pegboard or the ground. Handle them with tongs to avoid getting your scent on them. The remaining item you will rub so it gets your scent, and then throw it among the other unscented ones (which are firmly anchored to the ground) and tell him "find mine!" If he tries to pick up an unscented item, it won't budge because it's wired into place. He'll only be able to pick up the scented item, and he'll soon learn that's the only rewarding one to retrieve. Because, of course, you'll be rewarding him with heaps of praise and tidbits when he brings it to you.

Once he's no longer even trying to pick up the unscented items you can start having fun by challenging him with all sorts of items in all sorts of places. Including your car keys.

## SCUBA DOG
### *RETRIEVING UNDERWATER*
**Abilities:** Fetch, swim

Not every dog will take to this activity, but those that do, love it! You have to start with a dog who loves to retrieve. A love of water helps, too, but that may develop with experience. Although you can use any sinkable item, the best underwater retrievable is a rubber toy available at most pet stores that is made up of three arches. That means the toy rests on two of the arches while the third one is elevated so the dog can easily grasp it. But you can start with dog treats or favorite toys.

You can use a large bowl as your pool at first, but you'll eventually want to graduate to a kiddie pool and then a real pool or lake. Start with the item in just a couple of inches of water. Gradually increase the depth, giving your dog a chance to learn how to exhale while his nose is under water. Make sure he's confident at one depth before advancing to deeper water. Several milestones must be accomplished: placing the nostrils under water, placing the eyes under water, placing the ears underwater, and finally, diving underwater.

Different dogs will choose different stopping points, but that's OK—you probably don't need your dog for an underwater recovery mission. Accept that he may not ever be comfortable submerging important parts of his anatomy. You can add other challenges by combining the underwater retrieve with other retrieving games. Can your dog retrieve several items one at a time? Can he retrieve an underwater item based on your directions? Can he combine scent discrimination with underwater retrieving by choosing which container of water holds the item you've scented?

## RIGHT ON THE MARK
### *RETRIEVING BY MEMORY*
**Abilities:** Fetch

Even if they never go hunting, many dogs love to learn the tricks of hunting retrievers. A busy hunting retriever may have to remember where several birds fell and bring back every one. Hunters call this marking, but you don't have to go hunting to enjoy this challenging game.

Warm up with a few throws where your dog can see exactly where the item lands. Then throw the retrieving item so it falls just out of sight, perhaps in tall grass or behind something. Your dog should have no problem finding and retrieving it. Next, hold him or have him sit and stay until the item has landed before sending him to retrieve it. As he gets better, make him wait slightly longer, up to 30 seconds. Now he is using his memory to find an item he saw land earlier but can't currently see.

But can he find two such items? Probably not at first, unless he can cram them both in his mouth. More likely he will run to one and then take it to the other and either trade items or stand there and wonder what to do. You need to show him how to bring them both back to you, one at a time.

If you used the hallway trick to teach him to fetch, you have a head start. That's where you sit in the middle of your hallway and throw a toy one way and when he brings it back, you immediately throw another toy the other way. That way he already understands the concept of bringing back something and immediately leaving for something else. But the hallway doesn't work for big dogs; there's just not enough room. Besides, you'll be throwing both items before he brings one back, which makes a big difference. Still, one concept remains: You need to make it impossible for him to get to the second item without going past you first. One easy way to do this is to stand at the corner of your house (or the outside corner of a fenced yard). Another, and more ambitious, way is to divide your backyard almost in half with temporary fencing and stand at one end of the fence.

In either case, you'll throw one item to one side of the corner or fence, and the other item to the other side. Let your dog watch both of them land. Send him first to get the item you threw second; this will make it easier for him. Encourage him to bring it back and, once he's given it to you, turn him to face the other object and send him for it. You may have to run part of the way with him if he seems confused.

As he gets more experienced you can back away from the fence or corner, leaving a gap between it and you. Call him toward you if he forgets and heads directly to the second item without first bringing the first one to you. It may take some practice—nobody said this was easy—but eventually he'll be able to do this in an open field. And that's when it's lots of fun. Then it's time to try three items—maybe even four. It *can* be done!

## BLIND DOG'S BLUFF
### FOLLOWING DIRECTIONS
**Abilities:** Fetch, sit, stay, heel, come

Real hunting retrievers have another talent that's also a lot of fun: the blind retrieve, in which they must depend totally on their handler's directions to find a bird that has fallen out of sight. It's not easy—but that's why it's fun.

Most people find a whistle helps them communicate with their dog at a distance. Start by teaching your dog to stop at one whistle tweet and come at a series of tweets. You'll also need to teach your dog some verbal signals and hand signals. The verbal commands commonly used are "back" (meaning move directly away from you) and "over" meaning move directly right or left. Hand signals are as follows:

- Arm extended straight up indicates "back."
- Arm extended straight to the side indicates "over"; extending the right arm tells the dog to run to your right, and extending the left arm tells the dog to run to your left.
- Arm extended at a 45-degree angle (between vertical and horizontal) tells the dog to run at an angle; extending the right arm tells the dog to angle to your right, and extending the left arm tells the dog to angle to your left.

How do you teach your dog all this? Here's one way retriever trainers use. Get three chairs or parking cones that you can carry with you and place in your yard. Set them up in a baseball diamond configuration, with the chairs or cones marking the positions of each base. Let your dog watch you toss several retrieving items to second base. Then take him to the pitcher's mound position, turn and face the item to retrieve. You can turn him with his collar, or better, have him heel so that he faces exactly the same direction you do. Either way, line up directly facing second base. When he is lined up correctly say "line," which he'll soon learn means he's facing where he should go. Then send him to retrieve with the command "back," followed by the command he already knows, "fetch." You want him to learn that "back" means to run directly away from you.

If he seems hesitant, you can run with him to second base and encourage him to retrieve the item. Regardless of whether you've had to run with him or not, when he returns to you with the item, run backwards a few steps so he runs farther toward you. Repeat this, getting gradually farther from second base until you're eventually sending him all the way from the home plate position.

Once your dog is running to second base reliably, it's time to send him to retrieve when he's not already at your side. Let him watch you place items at second base, but then put him on a sit-stay facing home plate. You should be a few steps in front of him, between him and home. This introduces him to the concept of facing you, and then twirling and running away from you on the "back" command. You will gradually increase the distance between him and you until you are at home plate while he's at the pitcher's mound, facing you and awaiting your directions.

Now comes the big test. Place the items at second base, but for the first time, don't let him see you put them there. Send him to retrieve. Suddenly your dog will be retrieving something without ever having seen it fall—relying totally on his confidence in you and your directions.

But what challenge is it for him to just run to second base every time? It's time to teach him right from left. Let him watch you toss several items to first base. Have him sit on the pitcher's mound facing you from your position a few feet toward home. Command "over," using a hand signal in which your arm is fully extended to the side toward first base. If he runs to second base out of habit, he won't find anything there, so start over and let him once again see you drop the items on first base. As he catches on, work your way back toward home plate, always sending him from his pitcher's mound position. Then do the same with third base. Then present him with a mixture of placements at first, second and third base positions. Wow!

One more skill is needed before you can direct your dog in the field. You must be able to make him stop. What if he started running or swimming on a "back" command, missed the retrieving object and just kept going? Besides, he needs to stop and look at you so he can see your next directional signal. To do this you want him to stop, turn and face you when told to. Practice with your dog on a long leash so that when he hears a single whistle tweet you can make sure he stops, faces you and sits. Do this by tweeting the whistle and then running back a few steps so he must stop, turn and then stop again. When he has the general idea, or at least knows that a tweet means to stop, take him off leash and send him from home plate to second base. As he crosses the pitcher's mound, stop him with a single tweet. If he doesn't turn to face you (and many dogs will do so naturally), call him in toward you so that he must turn, and then tweet for him to stop again. Then have him sit. When he is sitting and looking at you, send him to one of the bases for a retrieve.

Now you have a dog who will go straight out, straight in (come), stop, go right or go left according to your directions. It's time to go into the field and test his skills in high grass. This is a difficult game to learn, but it's a lot of fun and when you get through teaching all the steps, you may just want to take him to a hunting test (see page 143). At the very least, you'll want to show him off to all your friends!

## FIDO FIND AND FETCH

### SNIFF OUT AN ITEM
**Abilities:** Fetch

When fetch is too simple but marking and blind retrieving are too complicated, compromise with a fun game of find and fetch. This game challenges your dog to find a thrown item she hasn't seen land. Rather than follow your directions, she can just nose around and eventually come across it.

Once your dog is fetching enthusiastically, hold her as you throw her favorite retrievable object. Right before it lands, block her vision of it, either by placing your hands over her eyes or by throwing it so it lands around a corner or into deep grass. It helps at first if the object makes some noise as it lands. Before letting her go, make sure she is aimed right toward the area and, as you send her, say "get it!" and swing your arm toward the object.

Chances are she won't have much problem doing this. Gradually obscure her view a little bit earlier until she is relying entirely on the hints you give her: the direction you've faced her, your arm signal and your words "get it!" If she's having problems, make the object land in an easier place. Some dogs will search around for awhile and then give up. When that happens, quickly help her by aiming her toward the object and giving your arm signal and the words "get it!" once again. She needs to know that it's really out there!

Once she is confident the object is out there and she is no longer depending on you for help, you can start to hide it instead of tossing it. By doing this, you're replacing the big hint of knowing you've tossed the object with another possible hint: your scent trail. Send her by facing her toward the object and giving her some direction with your arm movement. Again, you may have to give her some hints, but it's a fine line between keeping up her confidence and allowing her to play you for a sucker.

The next step is to hide the object in different places and get her used to searching in the open, inside and even in cars. Can you say "sniffer dog"? Your dog now has the basic skills to start sniffer dog school.

## SNOOPY SNIFFER
### SNIFF OUT TROUBLE
**Abilities:** Fetch

Is your dog good at finding things? Perhaps she's a sniffer dog wannabe. But why should law-enforcement dogs have all the fun? You can help hone her sniffing skills, have some fun and search the kid's rooms with a little—well, a lot—of training.

Start by mastering the Fido Find and Fetch game. You've probably been using a ball, retrieving dummy or favorite toy. Now you have to decide what you want your dog to sniff out. Most sniffer dogs are trained to find a group of related objects, such as a family of fruits, drugs or explosives. Unless you're eager to search your garage for bombs, your car for contraband or your yard for cadavers, you should probably concentrate on something mundane like fruits or cheeses as your target scents. Otherwise it's doubtful your "training my dog" excuse will fly at your trial— especially when you try to demonstrate how gifted your sniffer dog is and she just stares at you blankly.

Once you've chosen your target scent (and we'll say it's cheese), attach a small sample to an item your dog is already retrieving. Professional sniffer dog trainers usually first teach the dogs to find hollow tubes that have lots of little holes for scent. They stick the target sample inside the tube, plug up both ends and practice hiding it. You could use a section of hose. Whether you start off with a toy or a tube, the concept is the same: by combining the scent of your target substance with the item she's already learned to find, she'll soon come to focus on the new scent as well. You can add to the game by hiding scented items in hard-to-find places, and by making the scent harder to smell by enclosing the item in plastic containers.

If you plan to eventually add more scents to your dog's repertoire, name each scent. As you send your dog for it, say the scent's name just before you say "find it!" as in "cheese . . . find it!" Although it seems more grammatically correct to say "find the cheese!" dogs aren't great grammarians. They're better at learning to predict things, and when they hear "cheese" they learn that "find it!" follows. Pretty soon they don't even wait to hear "find it!" any more; they just start looking. Introduce new scents in the same way, attaching them to an item your dog already knows how to retrieve, then gradually diminishing the strength of the scent.

You may even be able to teach your dog the scent of familiar items such as your slippers or the newspaper, and teach her to retrieve those by name. Teach these the same way, by attaching them to a familiar retrieval item and saying "slippers . . . find it!" Not only is this handy when you're lounging in your easy chair at home, but if you've taught your dog to find your keys, she may be able to find them when you can't.

## HOT ON THE TRAIL
### *TRACKING YOU DOWN*
**Abilities:** None

Do you get lost in your own backyard? Teach your dog to track you down. It's easier than it seems. Your dog already knows how to use her nose; you just need to give her a little direction. The hardest part will be finding a section of your yard that isn't already drenched in your scent. Try to refrain from entering at least part of your yard during the training phase, so that you don't leave confusing scent trails.

You can train your dog by yourself, but it's easier to work with a friend who can hold your dog while you lay the trail and hide. To train by yourself, start by walking in a straight line for about 20 feet. Drop a small dog treat every few feet—sort of like leaving a trail of bread crumbs. Place a bigger pile of treats at the end of the trail. Then retrace your steps to where your dog is.

Say "track!" and point to the ground where your trail is. You may have to help direct your dog from treat to treat at first. Keep repeating this part of the game, but gradually walk a longer distance and leave a bigger space between the dropped treats. Be sure you either retrace your exact steps every time you leave a trail or use a totally new part of the yard. Don't be discouraged; it often takes a long time before dogs realize they can find the treats by following your scent trail.

When your dog can find the treats when they are 15 feet apart, add a right-angle turn to your track. Eventually you can drop fewer and fewer treats and add more turns and distance. If you have a friend to help, you can hide at the end of the trail and have your dog find you. Be sure to have lots of treats and praise ready for your dog when she tracks you down!

If your dog tries to act like you've asked the impossible, remind her of this: Dogs have followed human trails as old as 105 hours and have trailed for distances as long as 135 miles. She can follow your two-minute-old trail for 50 feet.

You can devise all sorts of challenges for your backyard Bloodhound. Dogs use several clues when they track. They smell not only you and the scents on you (actually, the scents that have fallen off you), but also the vegetation you've crushed as you walked on it. That means trailing you over different surfaces, especially ones without vegetation, can be tough. Play the role of escaping prisoner and see if you can outfox her by laying your scent trail over asphalt, water and sand, or across the path of other pedestrians.

## BACKTRACK

### A HANDY FIND-IT GAME
**Abilities:** Trail

A skill that can be particularly handy is to teach your dog to backtrack along your trail when you've been walking and dropped an item. Start by walking with your dog and dropping the item so your dog sees it drop. Then, after a few paces, act surprised and worried, say "backtrack!" and turn back to search. Send him to help search, and praise him when he finds it before you do. Gradually lengthen the time between dropping it and discovering it missing, and then send your dog after it when he didn't get to see it fall. When your dog finds the item, let him know he's your hero!

## SOMEONE'S WATCHING YOU
### HOW TO MAKE YOUR DOG FEEL PARANOID
**Abilities:** None

There's nothing quite as unnerving as the knowledge that you're being watched. Dogs are no different when it comes to being spied on! This is a game to be played inside or in your fenced yard, because a few dogs can get scared and try to run away. Most dogs, however, will see the humor and enjoy the tingle of excitement that comes with being the object of a stalking.

Wait until your dog is distracted and is not watching you. Then sneak away and hide in a poor hiding place. Once hidden, let your dog "discover" you peeking out at him. If you're behind a tree, make a suspicious noise to get him to look your way, then let him catch just a glimpse of you before ducking back behind it. Some dogs will come right over to investigate, nuzzling your hands to see what you have for them. These dogs probably won't be much fun for this game. Other dogs will come close then become cautious and stop. Others won't even take a step toward you, preferring to stand straight and use their X-ray vision to peer through the tree.

If the dog moves to the side to get a better look at you, just slowly move to keep the tree between you. Move slowly. That makes you seem creepier. You can run from tree to tree, or come out in plain view and creep toward your dog. For optimal creepy effect, bend over at the waist and put your hand over your face, peering through your fingers. Stop if your dog seems truly upset and let him know it's just you playing a game. He will most likely act like a kid who has just been on a roller coaster—giddy with relief!

You can play this evil game in the house as well, but make sure your dog has an escape route and that it's not over a slick floor. Know your dog well enough to know when to quit, or when to not start at all. Pushing a dog to the point of real fright is a good way to make him bite—and you will have only yourself to blame. If you're trying to raise a good watchdog, this is not the way. Teaching him that people creeping around and hiding usually turn out to be you just goofing is poor training for a sentry. By the same token, don't allow nonfamily members, or even children, to play this game. It's asking for trouble. Don't play it with dogs with aggressive or shy tendencies.

This sounds like a weird game to enjoy, but it's one of my dogs' favorites. And if you take a camera with you, you can get some great photos of your dog standing at full attention looking right into the camera.

## KEEP-AWAY
### THE OLD FAVORITE
**Abilities:** None

Dogs love to play keep-away. You can practically hear them giggling as you lunge to grab their prize and they pull it just out of reach. True, you'd be foolish to teach this game to a dog you want to use as a reliable retriever (a dog playing keep-away with a bird would never be invited back for a day in the duck blind), but most of us don't have such aspirations. By using words that tell your dog when the game is beginning and ending, you can separate it from everyday life and make it clear it's not up to him to decide to start playing.

You can also use a special toy that is dedicated only to playing keep-away. Give him that toy, say "thief! thief!" and give chase. At first he may think you're serious and stop in his tracks, so you may have to combine it with tug-of-war or other chasing games to build his confidence. When the game is over, say "you're under arrest" and ask that he bring you the toy. If he does, reward him. If he doesn't, simply turn and walk away. Game over.

Letting him know that even keep-away has rules helps prevent him from playing keep-away with your car keys when you're late for work.

## CATCH ME IF YOU CAN
### YOU CHASE HIM . . .
**Abilities:** Come

One of the most popular games dogs play with each other is the game of catch-me. They delight in being either the chaser or the chasee. Most dogs are more comfortable in the role of chasee when playing with people. Some trainers caution against play-chasing your dog for fear the dog will learn she can evade you. But most dogs already know you are as slow as a slug.

Before playing this game, you should teach your dog to come when called and you should use distinctive words to signal the beginning and end of the catch-me game. Begin the game with "I'm gonnagetyou!" and stalk your dog, pouncing at him. Give chase as best you can, but if he leaves you in the dust, either crouch down and wait for him to do a fly-by (when you can pounce at him once again) or turn around and run full blast the opposite way—a sure-fire way to get him headed back in your direction.

Some dogs like to see how close they can pass without hitting you. If you have one of these, stand perfectly still so you don't run into the dog's path. A high-speed collision with a dog is very dangerous for both of you. At the end of the game, give a game-over word such as "finished" and call the dog to you using his regular recall command. Give him a treat and take a break.

## BE THE BUNNY
### *HE CHASES YOU*
**Abilities:** Self-control

What about a game of catch-me where you're the one being chased? This is not the game for aggressive dogs or dogs who could get carried away and hurt you. It's also not an appropriate game for children to play with dogs. But for some dogs—dogs who are not prone to bite, get carried away or act dominantly toward people—it can be a fun and safe game.

The problem with playing keep-away from a dog is that you can't. Almost any dog can run you down, even on three legs. If your dog laughs as he flies past you, you can outsmart him by skidding on the brakes and changing directions just as he passes. Keep zig-zagging and backtracking at full speed, especially when he's not looking. You'll never get away, but you can try to at least reach a tree or other cover. Or just give up and give him a big hug when he catches you!

## PILLOW FIGHT
### DODGE BALL WITH MARSHMALLOWS
**Abilities:** None

A fun variation on the catch-me game is the addition of dodge ball. You can't throw a ball or anything hard or big at your dog— it's much too dangerous—but you can throw a soft marshmallow that will bounce right off. Some dogs delight in racing past as you throw marshmallows at them. You'll almost always miss, but even if you don't, they won't hurt a bit. The biggest danger is that she may double back to try to eat them, and risk ruining her figure. More seriously, she may try to eat and run at the same time, which could be a choking hazard. So you should try to pick up any marshmallows before she can grab them.

## LASSIE GO HOME
### A RACE TO THE FINISH
**Abilities:** Find home

What dog doesn't like to race? The hard part is letting him know where the finish line is. Most dogs know their home, and if they realize that a treat awaits, you can teach them that "go home!" means to race home. Start just a few feet from home, say "go home!" and run with your dog to the house. Give him a treat as soon as you get there. Increase your distance from home gradually, and then race your dog back home.

Your dog is probably faster than you are, so once he knows the game, it might be more fun to teach him to stay while you walk a little closer to home for a head start. Then yell "go home!" and take off! This game can only be played where it's safe to have your dog off-lead and no roads are near.

## OVERCOMING OBSTACLES
### A JUMPING GAME
**Abilities:** Jumping

Some dogs love to jump. Some love to jump over your fence, but others prefer to jump more acceptable obstacles. Too many people are careless when they encourage their dogs to jump. In some cases they unintentionally give the dog the confidence to jump the backyard fence. Make sure any jumps you practice with are not as high as your backyard fence and do not resemble the fence in any way. You can have plenty of fun with broad jumps and tire jumps that don't teach your dog to jump high. Instructions for making several types of jumps are on pages 178.

Jumping is not a tool for conditioning out-of-condition dogs. Fat dogs, lame dogs and old dogs should not jump at all. Puppies should jump no more than ankle height, because stresses can damage their growing bones and developing joints. Some breeds weren't designed to be jumpers. Consult your veterinarian for advice about your particular dog's jumping abilities.

Take-off and landing areas for jumps should always be on nonskid surfaces and landing areas should be soft. Jumps should have straight approach and post-landing paths so that dogs aren't twisting as they take off or land. Give your dog a day off between jumping days.

Remember that *fun* is the key word here. Pushing your dog to jump heights she's not comfortable jumping is scary, not fun, for her. Too many people are in too much of a rush to push their dog's limits. This sets the dog up for loss of confidence and possible physical harm. When asking your dog to jump higher and higher, ask yourself which one of you is getting the thrill out of it; chances are your dog will be happier jumping more comfortable heights.

Jumping is an acquired skill that requires conditioning and experience for correct execution and timing. It depends on the interplay of muscles and joints throughout the dog's body. Asking a dog to hurl herself over a high jump before she's had a chance to learn how to control her body is unfair, unsafe and uncomfortable. What kind of game is that?

Even after training, most of your jumps should be no more than your dog's shoulder height. This is high enough for her to put some effort into it but not so high that she is repeatedly pushing herself or pounding her front end on landing. If you do have one of the few dogs who enjoys aiming for the stars, always act as a spotter when she attempts a challenging height.

Although most jumping should be done off-leash, you can start the baby jumps with your dog on a leash. With your dog by your side, simply step over a low jump together. It's easiest if the jump goes all the way across a path, so your dog has no choice. Say "over!" and encourage her. As she builds confidence, you can increase speed so she begins to hop over the jump instead of stepping over it. If she likes to retrieve, throw a favorite toy so she can get a feel for jumping off-leash. Then raise the height and encourage her to jump over the new height. Even though she may be tackling this new height without problems, quit early. It will take awhile for her muscles to adjust to this new exercise.

Practice the broad jump in the same way. If you're using a jump made of separate pieces with spaces between them, you may need to have your dog run up to the jump quickly so she can't try to place her feet in the spaces. Remember to say "over!" so she doesn't confuse it with cavaletti (page 183), if you're also teaching that.

Start teaching the tire jump with the tire at ground level. Encourage your dog to walk through the tire. Once she's comfortable doing that, place the tire where she can't go around it and throw a toy through it. You want her to eventually race through the tire to get the toy. Only then should you raise the tire slightly off the ground. Continue to raise it slightly as your dog becomes more accomplished.

Once your dog is a joyous jumper, you can set up jump combinations. When doing so, remember that your dog needs ample room to get into position for and recover from each jump. Making impossibly difficult courses sets your dog up for refusals or injuries. Unless your dog is in training to save babies from burning buildings, there's no reason to put her through this sort of obstacle course. This is a game!

## SPRINKLER MADNESS
### FUN ON A DOG DAY AFTERNOON
**Abilities:** None

Take one hot day and one hot dog. Just add water. Then watch the fun begin as your pup pounces, barks, bites and digs at the water gushing from the end of the hose. And digs and digs in the mud until she looks like the creature from the black lagoon. Once she's had her mud bath, attach a sprinkler so the water is now airborne, and watch her bite and chase and run through the fountain. If you're lucky she'll wash herself off. More likely she'll just get gooier.

The warning for this game: If you have in-ground sprinklers, you may not want to encourage her to dig at them unless you want a perpetual geyser. And if she likes to carry the hose while it's gushing water, make sure she can't carry it into the house when you're not looking!

## HANG ON SNOOPY!
### TUG-OF-WAR
**Abilities:** None

Tug-of-war is one of those games that many dog trainers will caution you against playing with your dog. The reasoning is that it pits you against your dog and, at some point, you invariably allow the dog to win, giving him the idea he can best you in a battle of strength. For some dogs, this could create delusions of grandeur. Most dogs, however, already know you are helpless against them in any war of wills. They learned that when you gave them treats from the table or allowed them to push you to the little sliver of mattress on the side of the bed.

However, you can preserve the illusion that you're in control by adding a couple of elements to your game of tug-of-war. The way to do this is to first teach your dog to give you a toy when you ask. Ask nicely "may I?" and offer to exchange a treat for the toy. Repeat this until your dog learns to trade the toy for a treat whenever you ask. Now you have a way to end a tug-of-war game in a draw, simply by asking your dog to give you the toy. You also have a way to start the game by using a special tug toy that you bring out just for this game. Tell him "tug time!" and entice him to hold on by starting with gentle, quick tuglets.

Use common sense when you play tug-of-war. Don't jerk your dog's head back and forth or up and down; neck problems are not uncommon in dogs. Don't allow your dog to hang from his teeth; at least his hind feet should always be on the ground. If he has dental problems, this may not be the best choice of games.

And dog trainers are right when it comes to some dogs. Dogs who have a tendency to be aggressive or domineering with their people should find more cooperative games to play.

## FREQUENT FLYERS
### *FRISBEE CATCHING*
**Abilities:** None

Many people toss a Frisbee or some other type of flying disc at their dogs expecting that the dog will leap into the air and latch right onto it, only to have their dog duck and wince at the sight of the disc coming her way. Most dogs have to be taught how fun disc catching is. You don't teach them this by smacking them in the head with a disc thrown at them, though. You teach them in little steps and with soft discs made just for dogs.

Start by getting your dog interested in the disc. Encourage her to grab it and play with it. Hold it in the air around her nose level and let her practice grabbing it as you twist and turn it. Have her leap up just a little so she is jumping to grab it from you. Then roll the disc on its side and encourage her to chase it. You want her to grab it as it rolls. Now you have a dog who can grab a moving disc from your hand and a spinning disc on the move. Then combine the two by encouraging your dog to grab it from your hand, but tossing it a few feet just as she leaps for it. She'll probably leap just a little more so she can grab it only inches from your hand—her first midair catch! As she gets the idea, you can throw it slightly farther.

Around this time you'll start wishing you had perfected your throwing skills so the disc will hang in the air longer. You need to practice your throwing; after all, you can't expect your dog to be a consistent catcher if you're not a consistent thrower. As your skills increase, so will your dog's.

You've probably seen dogs jumping and twisting and somersaulting to catch discs thrown high in the air. For most dogs, this is not a good idea. Yes, it will impress people at the dog park. But it will also make your dog susceptible to many injuries, some of which can be serious. If you wish to work on advanced tricks, join a disc dog group so you can get personalized guidance. If you must show off and don't have such a group, and if your dog is fairly lightweight, you can try a vault in which you bend over so the dog can leap off your back to catch the disc. This is taught by first teaching her to jump over your leg at ground level as you throw while sitting, and building to jumping over your raised leg as you throw while standing, as well as your raised arm while kneeling. You'll have to reposition her each time so she starts well away from you to get your timing right. Finally, kneel with one leg bent at the knee. You want to encourage your dog to use your bent leg as a take-off point by throwing the disc so that she needs your leg for height. It will take awhile for her to feel comfortable jumping on you like this, so when she does, praise her exuberantly.

## CANINE WORLD CUP
### SOCCER FOR DOGS
**Abilities:** Chase ball

Canine soccer works pretty much the way you think it would: You can only use your feet, and your dog can use whatever she wants. Of course, if you break the rule about not using your hands, nobody's going to know. There is one additional rule: You cannot under any circumstances kick your dog. That means that when she is going for the ball, you may only be able to play defense.

Try different balls. Some dogs are talented at attacking fully inflated balls and making them bounce all around. Others prefer a deflated ball they can grab in their mouths. This game really has no goal net and, in fact, no goal at all except the chance to get out and play ball with your dog.

## JUMP AND BUMP
### CANINE VOLLEYBALL
**Abilities:** Catch

You can teach your dog to play volleyball. Start by teaching her to leap up and catch balls. Then substitute a lightweight ball or even a balloon (as long as she can't bite it and pop it!), so when she tries to catch it she bumps it with her nose instead and sends it flying back up. Keep tossing the ball to her and when she hits it, bat it back. Try to get a volley going. Then add a low net. Finally, challenge another human-canine volleyball team to a game.

## SPELUNKING WITH SPOT
### BACKYARD TUNNELING
**Abilities:** None

Most dog games assume dogs want to fetch and do tricks. Many dogs do, but many other dogs are turned on by doing what they were bred to do. For terriers, that often means going underground. Even nonterriers can enjoy the canine version of spelunking.

You can start making your dog feel comfortable about going through enclosed spaces by enticing her to follow a toy dragged by a string. Place a couple of cardboard boxes on their sides with the tops and bottoms removed, and just pull the toy through slowly as she follows. Let her catch the toy and then have a good game of tug-of-war. When she's running through the makeshift boxes without hesitation, it's time to move to a better tunnel.

Depending on your dog's size, you may be able to buy a five-foot section of drainpipe and secure it on top of the ground. If that won't work, you can use straw bales to fashion tunnels in your yard, or you can make your own tunnels (or liners, as they are called) using wood for the sides and top and keeping the natural earth floor. Start with the liners above ground and use only a short, straight section. Then gradually add more distance and a turn or two.

If your liner has a removable top you can run a string through the tunnel with a toy on it and lure your dog through. If you really don't mind destroying your yard (and let's face it, your dog has probably already done that for you) you can sink your liners into the ground so the tops are flush with ground level. But a warning: This only works on high ground; otherwise the tunnels will be flooded with the first good rain. Note, too, that this may well be the final step in convincing your neighbors that you are more than a little odd.

Serious terrier people often keep rats as pets and have them earn their keep by providing eau de rat for the tunnels. Mix used rat bedding with water and then spray it along the tunnel path. This provides a powerful lure to rodent-crazed dogs. Serious terrier people also ask their rats to lounge in a cage at the end of the tunnel to give their dogs an added incentive. They never allow the rat to become stressed or harmed, however. Even so, not everyone is anxious to add a pet rat to the family, and they can substitute a treat trove as an incentive at the end of the tunnel.

It's tempting to give your dog a nudge, or even a shove, to get her started into the tunnel, but being pushed into a closed space is alarming for any dog and will only result in greater reluctance to enter. When your dog does get to the goal, reward her by letting her bark momentarily at the caged rat or eat all the treats.

Once your dog is charging through the tunnel without hesitation, shorten the tunnel and introduce a turn at the very beginning. At first the turn should be only a foot from the entrance of the tunnel, so she can practically see the daylight through the other end by poking her head way in and peering around. Soon she will understand that lack of daylight just means another turn is up ahead. Keep adding more turns and tunnels.

## PULLING HIS WEIGHT
### TOTE THAT BARGE
**Abilities:** Stay, come

How often have you struggled to haul heavy loads of dirt and other gardening stuff around the yard while your ever-so-helpful dog volunteers to carry your gloves—and then expects to be praised for all his hard work. Sure, fetching can be handy, but pulling is invaluable! And many dogs love the chance to test their strength.

However, some dogs are just too polite to pull. Chances are you've worked hard to teach your dog not to pull when he's on leash. The first step is to buy a harness for your dog. He will soon learn that when he's in harness he's not only allowed, but expected, to pull. You can get a custom-fitted harness from one of the harness makers linked to the International Weight Pull Association website (see page 159). The custom fit enables your dog to pull harder with greater comfort. You can also buy or build a cart if you want to go whole hog, but you don't have to.

You may be content to have your dog pull a few items around, or you may wish to challenge your dog to feats of strength. As with most training and conditioning, the secret to weight training is to start slowly and avoid letting your dog fail. A dog who's used to succeeding tries to succeed. A dog who's used to failing gives up. Even if your dog is a strong dog capable of pulling you down the street, start him off with a light load. A cinder block or a tire works well for a large dog. Your goal at this point is to teach him the concept of pulling when asked to do so, not to test his strength.

If your dog already knows how to stay and come, you're ahead of the game. Attach his harness to the tire, walk him forward so there's no slack in the line, tell him to stay, walk in front of him and say "pull! come!" and encourage him to come to you. When he does, praise him lavishly. Continue to practice until you can call him from 15 feet away.

A well-trained and well-conditioned dog will understand what's being asked of him and will pull more decisively. He will be less likely to injure himself because he won't be lunging against his harness. He will have learned how to use his body effectively, pulling slowly, steadily and strongly. Your dog needs to develop his strength and stamina before tackling greater weights. Take your dog for a brisk walk while he drags a tire. (Maybe do this at night to avoid too many weird looks.) Once he's strutting along easily, add slightly more weight. Your dog should be conditioned using long walks with lightweight loads before asking him to try his first heavy weight pulls.

Add extra weight by adding additional tires or packing tires with bricks. When working with heavy weights, build up gradually. Remember, the heavier the weight, the shorter the distance you should ask of your dog. Make your dog stop while he still feels like a winner. Start with only a couple of pulls per day and don't weight train every day. Muscles need a chance to recuperate after weight training; challenging them every day tends to break them down, not build them up.

## SPECIAL DELIVERY
### A MESSENGER GAME
**Abilities:** Come

In World Wars I and II dogs were often used to deliver messages over long distances through enemy lines. They started their training in easier surroundings, however, and that's how you can train your dog to make special deliveries.

For this game you need two people and one dog who likes both of you well enough to search you out. Your dog will be a messenger and deliver secret messages (or dog treats) from one of you to the other. You can go all the way and make a secret pouch in his collar for him to hold the goods, or if he likes to retrieve, you can have him carry a pouch in his mouth.

Let your dog see you place the message or treat in the pouch. This will become a signal to him that the game is about to begin. Then hold him by the collar while your friend starts to run away. Tell your dog "special delivery!" and release him, just as your friend begins to call him. When he catches up your friend should praise him, take the pouch from his collar and give him a treat.

Now the friend places a new prize in the collar and you begin to run away. Your friend directs the dog "special delivery!" and encourages him to run after you. When he reaches you, remove the pouch and praise and reward him.

Gradually increase the distance, even until the target person disappears around a corner or goes out of sight before the other person releases the dog. Most dogs can turn the corner and find their person, but returning to the original person—now sight unseen around the corner—can be the first stumbling block for many dogs. Your dog may need to be taken to the corner and sent to his target person once he sees her.

One corner is all many dogs can manage. But some dogs are natural born messengers, and you can challenge them with increasing distances and varied terrain. To work over long distances, the target person should remain stationary while the other person walks the dog far away before releasing him. That person may need to run alongside the dog back to the target person at first. As the dog gains confidence he should gradually be able to find his way on his own. Again, once he reaches the target person, that person praises, rewards and sends him back to the original person. Now you have a dog who can run back and forth along a path and deliver messages from one person to the other. But you can make it harder.

The next challenge requires your dog to use his nose to sniff out the target person, who will have moved slightly away and out of sight from where the dog last saw her. The dog can use his memory to run back to the original place, but must then sniff around or follow a trail to find the person. See page 27 for tips on teaching your dog to trail. Here's another challenge: Can your dog deliver messages to different people you identify by name?

The messenger game is great for burning off energy and pounds—for both you and your dog! It's also handy if you want to be lazy around the house: Just have your dog deliver messages from one room to another.

## Chapter 3

# The Best Party Games

What's the best way to get to know those dog park folks you only refer to as "Sheba's parents," meet the cute guy who walks his dog down the block, or butter up the neighbor who seems suspicious about all those weird things you do with your dog? Throw an animal party for your party animal and his friends! Halloween, Valentine's Day, Groundhog Day, even Obedience School Graduation Day—any holiday is a good excuse for a Fido fest.

You don't need a canine caterer, but you do need to make some preparations. Have lots of small dog biscuits, treats and toys for prizes. If you're brave, bake a liver cake for your guests. Make a separate (nonliver) cake for the people guests, though. And be sure to send everybody home with a doggy bag.

You do have to be somewhat selective about your guest list. Some dogs are party-poopers (well, poopers can come as long as the party is outdoors). Dogs who behave aggressively toward people or other dogs are usually best partying alone. Overly excitable dogs should stick to calmer games or stay on-leash, and they should be kept away from much smaller dogs. Not every dog has to compete in every game.

When choosing party games, remember games aren't contests to see which dog can endure the most hardship. Games that revolve around resisting temptation or performing unsavory tasks are torture, not fun, for dogs. A few games are included here that emphasize obedience or self-control, but these shouldn't make up the entire party agenda. Mix it up!

The best parties include games that have no winners at all or that give dogs of different abilities chances to win. If a dog still can't win, make up a game just for him—and don't forget the old standbys of longest tail, longest tongue, most wrinkles, sexiest butt (is there such a thing on a dog?), biggest lapdog, longest drool, funniest, slowest, best costume, worst trick and dog-owner look-alike. Every dog is the best at something!

# THE GAMES

## LEADER OF THE PACK
### *FOLLOW THE LEADER*
**Abilities:** Walk on a leash

Here's a game suited for puppies who don't know any fancy tricks yet. It's just a simple game of follow the leader. Each person (along with her dog) gets a chance to play leader, and the rest of the guests follow the leader around obstacles, over baby jumps, through wading pools, up and down stairs and across different flooring surfaces—whatever looks like fun.

For more experienced dogs, the path could go over agility obstacles (see page 133), or the leader could have her dog perform a trick that the others can try to copy. Change leaders each minute; you want every leader to have a chance to try something none of the others has yet thought of. In this game nobody loses; everybody wins!

## A BARREL OF FUN
### *THE CANINE VERSION OF BARREL RACING*
**Abilities:** Run on- or off-leash alongside a person

Why should horses have all the fun? Here's the canine version of the popular rodeo barrel race. I hope you're in shape. . . .

Since most people don't happen to have barrels sitting around the house, you can use four chairs or trash cans instead. Arrange them in a square as far apart as you can reasonably expect people to run. Mark out a route that makes a cloverleaf pattern around them.

Each dog and handler has to run the marked route as quickly as possible, with the dog either on- or off-leash. They are timed from the start to the point at which the last member of the pair crosses the finish line.

This is a good game for kids and their dogs or for adults who want to experience the endorphin rush of a twisted ankle.

## WAGGING THE DOG
### A TALE OF THE TAILS
**Abilities:** Wag the tail

Here is a fun game that encourages people to loosen up and think about what makes their dogs happy. The object of the game is simple: The dog who wags her tail the most, wins.

Each person must get their dog's tail wagging while not using any words the dog knows and without teasing the dog with treats or toys. You can restrict words to particular categories such as "breeds of dogs," so people can only say things like "Dachshund! Chihuahua! Great Dane!" This way the dog responds only to her person's body language and tone. An impartial observer will need to count the number of wags—or in the case of tailless dogs, butt-wiggles—in a minute.

## SMOOCHY POOCHY
### A DOG KISSING CONTEST
**Abilities:** Lick person's face

Do you believe in public displays of affection? Then this contest is for you. The rules are simple, really. An impartial observer counts the number of licks your dog delivers to your face in one minute. You can talk baby talk, make kissy-kissy sounds or hold your dog up to your face—but you can't hide food in your mouth or smear your face with bacon grease. Come on, cheating at a dog kissing contest? That's just sad.

## Six-Legged Obstacle Course
### A RELAY RACE FOR DOGS AND PEOPLE
**Abilities:** Run on- or off-leash, jump simple obstacles, sit and stay

Who says dogs get to have all the fun? In a six-legged obstacle course relay, both dogs and people have to perform. In some cases, dogs and handlers will have to tackle the same obstacle at the same time—for example, wading through a kiddy pool or jumping a low hurdle together. In other cases, dogs will do a doggy-type obstacle or trick, then sit and stay while their person does a human-type obstacle or trick. Since you can make the human challenges really dumb, this is a great game for breaking the ice or humiliating your (former) friends.

## Sleuth Hound
### A SCAVENGER HUNT WITH DOGS
**Abilities:** Walk or run on a leash

This is a fun game for dogs who enjoy just running around aimlessly with their people rather than focusing on obedience skills. It's the same adventure as a traditional scavenger hunt, except you'll work in teams of at least two dogs and two people. All the teams are given the same list of items to find and bring back to the base. Of course, the items should have a dog theme. They could include a dogwood leaf, a hot dog bun (since you'll never make it back with the actual hot dog), a dog-eared book or an advertisement featuring a dog. Just make sure you don't make the list too unreasonable in warm weather. You want your dogs to come back ready to play more party games, not panting and wilting.

Even more fun is to have a picture hunt. Each team will need an instant photo or digital camera. They're given lists of locations or objects they must find, and all the dogs must be pictured at each location or with each object. To make it even harder, add the stipulation that the picture must show the dogs and people doing something in particular, such as sitting or holding a ball. So a list might include things such as "find a statue and have a ball," "go jump in the lake" or "become a tree-hugger." Sometimes leaving the exact instructions a little obscure and open to interpretation adds to the fun, especially when you're all looking at the pictures. You may have to set up certain items in some locations, substituting a gnome yard ornament for a statue or a wading pool for a lake. But that, too, only adds to the fun.

Give everyone an unreasonably short time limit—you don't want to make it too easy! Award each team one point per location or object successfully photographed. An additional point may be awarded for especially imaginative or gutsy photos. Late returners have their scores docked. The team with the most points wins. If you're using a digital camera, you can make copies of all the pictures so team members can take their pictures home.

## Bobbing for Bow-Wows
### A TREAT-BOBBING GAME
**Abilities:** Pick up floating or sunken objects from water

Here's the canine version of bobbing for apples. Since no self-respecting dog is going to get his muzzle wet for an apple, all you need to do is substitute dog biscuits, hot dog slices or other treats. Experiment to find some that float on top, some that float just below the surface and some that sink.

If you're having a summer pool party, you can use a child's wading pool and let each dog splash around after the treats. For more formal affairs (and what formal party would be complete without a bobbing contest?) you can use a large bowl or pot. There's a reason you don't just fill up your bathtub, though: One sight of it filled with water and all your doggy guests will head for the exit, sure you have a dreaded bath planned!

Fill your pool or bowl with lukewarm water. If you're using a bowl or pot, change the water between contestants; if you're using a pool just empty it after the entire contest. Let each dog have a practice bob until he gets one treat. Then start the clock and see how many he can grab in two minutes. Can anyone get them all?

A variation on the theme for ball-crazy dogs is to fill a kiddie pool with tennis balls. See how many balls each dog can pick up and give to his person in one minute. The person is allowed to get in the pool and encourage the dog in any way, and she can take each ball from the dog as soon as the ball is totally out of the water. The person can even help by picking up balls herself—of course, using only her teeth. Fair is fair.

Winners of this contest can be rented as pool boys to keep the neighbors' pools free from dog bones, hot dogs and tennis balls.

## SPOT SAYS
### *THE CANINE VERSION OF SIMON SAYS*
**Abilities:** Perform some basic obedience and tricks

Remember Simon Says? In that game, a leader, Simon, barks out orders that the rest of the people must quickly follow. It sounds easy, but if the order isn't preceded by "Simon says . . . " anyone who still followed it is kicked out. Spot Says works the same way, except that what Spot says, you must get your dog to do.

Spot (who is really a person) may call upon the dogs and handlers to do a mixture of fun and serious things, such as "Have your dog sit," "Get your dog to wag her tail," "Leave your dog on a stay while you turn in a circle five times clucking like a chicken," or "Kiss your dog on the lips." The catch, of course, is that the handlers must not tell their dog to do it unless Spot has preceded the command with "Spot says . . . ." Anyone messing up is out. The last dog and person team left is the winner.

## ROWDY RECALL RELAY
### *A RECALL RELAY RACE*
**Abilities:** Come when called

This is a fun relay that requires only that contestant dogs come when called. Of course, that's a pretty big "only" in the excitement of a dog party!

Divide the group into two or more teams, each with at least three members. If one team has more members than the others, designate one dog to run twice. Now have each team split up, with half on one side of the yard and the other half on the other side. Here's the important part: Each person is on the opposite side of the yard from her dog. Another team member will hold the dog until his owner calls.

At the "go!" signal, the first dogs on each team are released just as their owners start to call them. You can call repeatedly or do whatever it takes to get your dog running to you, as long as you don't cross in front of the start/finish line on your side. If you must do that, a five-second penalty is added to your time.

The next dog on your team gets released as soon as you have your dog by the collar. He, too, races across to his owner. The relay continues until each dog has run.

Of course there's an advanced version. In this version the dogs aren't held by other team members but are left on a sit-stay. If a dog breaks his stay, his person must place him back in the stay before he can be called again, and he can only be called when his person is back behind his own start/finish line. To make it even harder, the next dog in line can't start until the dog before is sitting in front of his person. If he does, the team gets a five-second penalty.

## THE GREAT EGG RACE
### AN EGG AND SPOON RELAY RACE WITH DOGS
**Abilities:** Walk on a leash

This is one time you'll wish you'd taught your dog to heel. The object of this game is to run an obstacle course with your dog on a leash. The course should be simple and clearly marked. It could include a simple slalom slope, a five-second pause spot and perhaps a few temptations along the way. That's not so hard, now, is it?

Except there's one more thing: You have to hold your dog's leash with one hand, and in that same hand you must also hold a spoon, and in that spoon you must also hold a hard-boiled egg. If you drop the egg, you have to go back to the starting line and do it all again.

It gets even better. To really do this game right you need two such obstacle courses, side by side. Divide your contestants into two teams and have a relay race. And remember, if you break an egg, the next dog in line is probably going to try to stop to eat it—and then your team is really in trouble. Egg on the ground equals egg on your face!

## UNDERWATER RELAY
### AN EVEN TOUGHER RELAY RACE
**Abilities:** Heel

Here's a variation of the egg race for people who are really confident about their dogs' heeling ability. Fill a tub with water. Place an empty tub with a "fill to here" mark in it 20 feet away. Each team is given an empty pie tin or other shallow container. At "go!" the first person on a team will dip the pie tin into the water. They must then hold the pie tin, along with their dog's leash (attached to the dog) over their own head as they proceed to the empty container across the yard. When they get to the empty container, they will empty the water into it and then race back and give the pie tin to the next team member. The first team to fill their container and make it back to the start wins. Just hope your dog doesn't decide to drink the water!

## WET T-SHIRT CONTEST
### THE RACE TO GET DRESSED
**Abilities:** Tolerate wearing clothes

OK, I added the "wet" part just to get your attention. Your dog doesn't have to be particularly well-trained for this contest—just amazingly tolerant. This is a dress-up relay race performed on a leash. You can go to thrift stores and buy an assortment of old clothes that should fit (sort of) the dogs who will be participating. Get T-shirts, socks or booties and hats (choose hats with tie strings). Place them all in a pile on the floor.

Divide  teams so that each team has the same number of small, medium and large dogs, if possible. Try to have at least three dogs on each team.

At the signal "go!" the first person and dog of each team race across the room to the clothing pile. Each person selects one piece (or a pair, if footwear) of clothing and puts it on her dog.

As soon as the dog is dressed the pair races back to the next team members. The first person then removes the clothes from her dog and gives them to the next person, who must put them on his dog. Once dressed, the second pair heads back to the clothing pile and the person adds another article to the dog's ensemble. Each succeeding dog has to wear the previous dog's outfit plus one additional item. If the teams are large, you can skip the requirement of wearing the previous dog's outfit. The winner is the team that completes the relay first.

## TOSS YOUR COOKIES
### A TREAT-CATCHING CONTEST
**Abilities:** Catch treats

So your dog can catch a treat. Can she do it under pressure? Here's a contest to find the champion treat catcher. Line up the contestants so they are at least 10 feet apart from one another. You don't want more than one dog lunging for an errant cookie. You may wish to have a helper for each dog to hold them on a loose leash so they don't wander into another dog's territory.

Place marks on the floor in front of each dog at 2, 4, 6, 8, 10, 15 and 20 feet. At the "go!" signal each person tosses a treat to her dog, beginning at the two-foot mark and working backward, mark by mark. If a treat hits the floor, the person has to start over at the two-foot mark. The first team to make a catch from the 20-foot mark wins. In case of a tie, you can keep moving back and award the prize to the team that can catch over the longest distance.

## HAVE A BALL
### A BALL-CATCHING CONTEST
**Abilities:** Catch a ball or flying disc

You're going to need a lot of balls to play this game—or a lot of flying discs. The challenge is simple: How many balls or discs can your dog catch in one minute? You will throw the balls or discs from a predetermined distance (10 to 20 feet usually works well), and keep throwing until your minute is up. Then the next team will try to beat your record.

## TOY DOGS
### A TOY-RETRIEVING CONTEST
**Abilities:** Recognize and retrieve toys

You'll need a small pile of dog toys, plus each person brings two of her dog's own toys. All the toys except those of the person who is competing are placed on the floor. At the signal "go!" the person throws one of her dog's toys into the middle of the pile and asks her dog to go get it. When he brings it back, she throws the dog's other toy. The object is to see how many toy retrieves your dog can do in 30 seconds, alternating the dog's own two toys.

If he brings back somebody else's toy, it doesn't count and you have to run out and get the toy he didn't retrieve, while simply putting aside the wrong toy. If your dog consistently brings back other dogs' toys, maybe he's trying to tell you something. You may need to schedule a trip to the dog toy store.

## POOCH PUISSANCE
### A HIGH JUMP COMPETITION
**Abilities:** High jump safely off-leash

Equine jumping competitions sometimes include puissance, which is a contest to see which horse can jump the highest. Dogs can do the same. This is not a contest for dogs who are not already conditioned for high jumping. But for a group of experienced and well-conditioned jumping dogs it can be a fun competition.

Just as with any high jump, the jump must be set up so that it collapses if the dog hits it. The landing surface must be soft (a lush lawn is adequate) and there should be plenty of room before and after the jump. Dogs can have as much room as they need to get their speed up when approaching the jump, but they must compete off-leash.

Begin at a height all the dogs can jump, then work up gradually, eliminating any dog who refuses or knocks the jump over. The winner is the dog who jumps the highest. In a mixed group of dogs, you can also award a prize to the dog who jumps the highest compared to his own height.

Don't just limit yourself to high jumps. It's actually safer for everybody to compete at broad jumps. If you want to be devious, you can also make the people compete, and use the combined heights of the dogs' and owners' best jumps to determine the winners.

## BOWSER BOWLING
### A GAME OF FINESSE (SORT OF)
**Abilities:** Chase or retrieve a rolled ball

Here's a game where klutzy dogs have the advantage. It works just like regular bowling, only your dog is allowed to cheat. You'll need 10 empty plastic soda bottles to use as bowling pins. You'll also need a tennis ball or something slightly larger to use as a bowling ball. The object is to roll your ball toward the bottles, knocking them down if possible, and to send your dog after the ball in hopes she will knock down the rest of them. Just as in bowling, you get two chances to knock down all the pins. If you know how bowling is scored, you can do the same here. If not, just add up the number of pins knocked down.

## LUCKY DUCKY
### A CARNIVAL PRIZE GAME
**Abilities:** Pick a toy or ball from water, do a simple trick

Remember the carnival game where the little plastic duckies floated around in a moat and you simply fished one out? Each duck had a number on the bottom that corresponded to a prize—and everyone was a winner! For the doggy version, fill a kiddy pool or big tub with floating toys or tennis balls, each with a number on the bottom. Each dog takes a turn picking out a toy. Each number corresponds to a predetermined challenge, such as catching a treat, sitting or doing something cute. If he performs the trick, he gets to keep the toy. If he doesn't, the toy goes back in the tub and the next dog in line picks one. Every dog gets to pick again and again until he finally wins a toy—even if you have to make some of the challenges much easier on the second try.

## BARK-O-RAMA
### A BARKING CONTEST
**Abilities:** Bark when encouraged

How many times have you wished your dog would stop that infernal barking? You deserve some recognition for all those interrupted naps. Now your dog's barking can pay off in a barking contest.

First, go for barking freestyle. Each dog has one minute to bark as much as you can get him to. You can do anything to encourage him—you can even bark like a dog if that's what it takes. The winner is the dog who barks the most times in one minute. Give that dog a bone. And his owner some earplugs.

Some time during this competition it will dawn on you that you must be insane to encourage such behavior, and you'll be right. You can't expect your dog never to bark, but you can teach him *when* to bark by having him do it on cue. That's the object of this next game. But first, to teach your dog to bark on cue, you need to wait until your dog looks as though he will bark, then quickly say "speak!" and then praise him as soon as he barks and give him a treat. You may wish to place your dog in situations you know will encourage barking so you can speed up the process. Check out the resources on page xv for more in-depth general training instructions.

This game for well-mannered barkers requires teams of three dogs each. They won't just be barking randomly; instead, they'll be doing their Three Tenors imitation. Dog A will bark once, then stop. Then Dog B will bark once and stop. Then Dog C will bark once and stop. If they bark out of order or fail to stop barking, the team has to start that chorus over. The first team to complete three flawless choruses of A–B–C barks wins. Give them a bunch of bones!

## HUNT HIGH AND LOW

### AN EASTER EGG HUNT FOR DOGS
**Abilities:** Find hidden objects

Everybody loves an egg hunt, and you don't have to wait until Easter. You'll need lots of plastic Easter egg shells of different colors. Place different kinds of smelly treats inside them, then show the dogs the eggs and let them see that they contain treats.

Hide the eggs around the yard or, for even more fun, along a hiking trail. You might wish to hide eggs containing the best treats in more difficult locations. Owners are encouraged to search along with their dogs. When you find an egg, open it up and let your dog eat the bounty inside. Keep the plastic shell so you can tally up your finds at the end. You can hide certain colors in more difficult locations, and then assign higher point values to those eggs. The team with the most points wins. You can also hide a few dog toys along with the eggs. These are bonus finds; they don't count toward points but it's finders-keepers!

Sure, you can also just hide dog biscuits instead of Easter eggs, but the eggs are so much more festive.

## MUSICAL PAIRS
### MUSICAL CHAIRS THE HARD WAY
**Abilities:** Walk on- or off-leash, sit, stay

Here's a game to convince your dog you've been partying a little too hard. Perhaps that's why it's one of the most popular dog party games.

You'll need about five dog-handler pairs. You know the drill: You have one fewer chair than you have contestants. You turn on some appropriate doggy song and send the pairs marching around the chairs in a clockwise direction (dogs on the outside), following a circle you've drawn on the ground about five feet out from the chairs. Then you turn the music off. The handlers must scramble for the chairs but there's a catch—they have to have their dogs sit first (without touching the dogs), and then remain sitting outside the marching perimeter, before the handlers can head for the chairs. Only when the dog's butt is on the ground can her person's butt be on a chair. The last person has no chair and is eliminated. The contest continues, with one chair removed as each pair is eliminated, until only one chair remains—and the person who claims it is the winner!

That's the easy version. The hard version is the same except the music stays off for one minute at a time. If a dog gets up during that minute, her person has to go back to her and get her to sit and stay again. And while that person is up, somebody else can claim that chair. In fact, anybody can entice anybody else's dog to break the stay by bouncing balls or being distracting—but they can't call the dog by name or do anything to scare the dog. At the end of the minute, the person who happens to be standing is out and a chair is removed. Only play this version with steady dogs and forgiving friends.

## Red Rover
### Red Rover for dogs
**Abilities:** Sit, stay

What would a list of dog games be without a game of Red Rover? Finally, here's a game where the less energetic dogs have an edge. Here's how to play. Split into two teams and line up facing each other across the room. Have all the dogs sit and stay next to their people.

Now a person on Team A picks somebody on Team B and calls her name: "Red Rover, Red Rover, send Rita right over!" That's the cue for Rita to leave her dog's side and trot over to Team A's side, where she will give the person who called her a treat for his dog, and then stand behind that person.

Then a person from Team B calls over somebody from Team A. If they call over somebody who has a handler standing behind them, that handler steps up to take their place and stands beside their dog. Otherwise the dog sits by himself. Teams can call back their own team members once they've advanced to the front line. A team member can also call their own dog to them if they decide to defect and join the opposing team. But if they call the dog and he doesn't come, they are both eliminated.

In addition, if a dog breaks from his stay position, that dog and handler are out of the competition. But any members so dismissed can try to distract the remaining contestants by playing with their dogs in the area between the two teams. They can roll balls, practice recalls or do anything else that's fun, but they should be discreet with the treats; this is supposed to be a fun game, not a chance to tease the poor good dogs who are still staying.

The winning team is the one that still has contestants staying in place when all the members of the opposing team have been eliminated.

## Star Search
### A message delivery challenge
**Abilities:** Come when called, ignore other dogs

Here's a party game for up to five teams of one dog and two people each. It's based on the Special Delivery game (page 40). This means the dogs will carry a message or item either in their mouths or on their collars.

You'll need a large fenced area to guard against some of the dogs deciding to run off together. For beginner dogs, have the dogs with their handlers stand in a line about 10 feet apart from one another. Send their target person out about 20 feet. On the signal "go!" the dog is released and the target person runs away, encouraging the dog to follow toward a finish line another 20 feet away. When the target person and dog both reach the finish line, the person takes the message or item from the dog, rewards the dog, and then sends him back to the first handler carrying a new message. Each handler can call and encourage as much as they want and they can run backward, as well—but they can't run in front of their start or finish line. The first dog to complete three circuits is the winner.

For experienced dogs, things get much harder. Make a star pattern with the star points about 50 feet apart. This game works best with five dogs because each team starts at one star point. It begins by having each target person go to the opposite star point (the one along the leg angling slightly to the their right). At the word "go!" they call their dogs to them. As the dogs are running, the releasing handlers cut across to their left (clockwise) to the adjoining star point. The dog is then sent back to the releasing handler at the new position, and while this is happening the first target person is moving to the next clockwise point. The first team to complete a circuit wins!

This game has two aspects that make it harder than the beginner's version. First, the people are moving their positions between each leg. Second, the dogs are all running intersecting routes and must avoid and ignore one another. It's controlled chaos—if you're lucky.

## SCENT HURDLES
### A SCENT DISCRIMINATION RACE
**Abilities:** Jump low hurdles, retrieve an article with owner's scent

Here's a game for doggy Mensa parties. It's a relay in which two teams of dogs run down a straight course of low jumps to get to a group of retrievable articles. The dog must sniff out the one article that has her handler's scent on it, and run back with it over the hurdles. When the dog passes the start/finish line, the next dog in line does the same, this time finding the article handled by *his* person.

# H-O-U-N-D
## A CANINE CHALLENGE
**Abilities:** You never know

The game of H-O-U-N-D is played like the human basketball game of H-O-R-S-E (sort of). One person has her dog do something she thinks the next person's dog (on the opposing team) can't do. If the second dog can't do what the first dog did, the second dog's team gets the letter "H." But if the dog can meet the challenge, the first team gets the letter. The first team to get stuck with all the letters in HOUND loses. Every dog on each team has to take a turn, but some strategy is involved in deciding which dog will accept which challenge.

You can also play C-H-O-W-H-O-U-N-D with food, in which eating different types of foods is the challenge. You can use various fruits and vegetables, or weird foods like rice cakes, popcorn, cheese or whipped cream from the can—as long as they are healthy for every dog competing. Keep in mind that chocolate and onions can be toxic to dogs, and alcohol is strictly off-limits.

## SWING YOUR PAWDNER
## A CANINE COTILLION
**Abilities:** Heel

If you have a big turnout, why not have a hoedown complete with square dancing? Look up some square dancing moves on the Internet and choose some that your guests can do. Use your imagination to come up with new steps geared toward dogs. But don't make everybody dress funny. You want them to actually come back.

# Chapter 4

# The Best Canine Activities

Saturday morning and what's there to do? As much fun as it is to hang around the house and play games with your dog, sometimes you want to take your dog out and socialize a bit. You want to share a great time with your dog and others without devoting your entire weekend or even your entire day to it. A lot of people share those feelings, so it may not be as difficult as it sounds to find some canine weekend entertainment. You can go to classes, fund-raising events and informal get-togethers. You can even help others by taking your dog to visit people who need the love a dog can give. If nothing else, simply take a drive in the country. Your dog will love it just because he's with you.

# THE ACTIVITIES

## PUPPY PALS

### ARRANGE A PLAY GROUP

**Abilities:** Play well with others

One of the simplest and most rewarding events you can share with your dog is to form a play-group that meets regularly. Talk to people who walk their dogs in your neighborhood and make a date to walk together. Get a group together and meet regularly so you can talk as you walk. Your dogs will get to know one another and look forward to their walks together. Then consider meeting at each other's houses a few times a week. Let the dogs play together in the yard or have a party; you can use some of the games suggested in Chapter 3, "The Best Party Games." Or caravan to a dog park and let all the dogs run amok.

By having a group that meets regularly, you won't be tempted to skip a walk on days you feel lazy. You and your dog will make new friends and have more fun. And your dog will be better socialized because he has the chance to interact frequently with dogs and people.

## DO LUNCH

### DINE OUT WITH YOUR DOG

**Abilities:** Behave in public

In many European countries it's commonplace to see dogs snoozing under tables at pubs and cafés, and the idea is gradually catching on in the United States. Make a date to meet some friends and do lunch. Larger cities with outdoor tables are the most likely to welcome dogs, often furnishing water bowls and dog treats. Those that are located near parks or dog parks are especially popular. If no such establishment exists, approach one with a likely atmosphere and point out the business they would attract by cornering the Bowser bistro market.

After lunch, move on to visit one of the dog bakeries that are popping up all over the country. Here you can spoil your dog shamelessly with haute dog cuisine.

No such places? Pack a picnic lunch for both of you—or better yet, invite a couple of friends—and enjoy a lunch outdoors. Make your own doggy delights with some of the recipes on page 13.

## GET SOME CLASS
### GET A PHIDO PHD
**Abilities:** None

A mind is a terrible thing to waste. Especially a canine mind. Have you considered getting your dog an education? Basic socialization and obedience classes are good for any dog. They help your dog learn how to behave around other dogs and people, and they give you guidance for training your dog. Every dog should know some simple commands such as come, stay, sit, down and heel. Knowing them can make her safer and more welcome wherever she goes. Obedience class is also a place for you to discuss home behavior and training problems, to show off what you've learned that week and to meet people with similar interests. Your dog can make friends, too, and look forward to seeing her schoolmates.

You don't have to limit yourself to obedience class. Some communities offer puppy socialization classes so youngsters from single-dog households can learn to interact properly with other dogs. Your dog will be exposed to unfamiliar people and circumstances, so she can learn to take life in stride when she grows up and meets the world. Agility classes are tremendous fun—more like going to recess—but most classes require your dog know some very basic obedience before starting. More specialized classes may be available in advanced obedience, tracking, conformation, herding, protection or field work.

Not all classes are created equal. Ask about the instructor's experience and sit in on a class to see if you're comfortable with the training techniques. Classes that use harsh methods aren't going to be any fun and probably won't give you the results you're aiming for. If you have an unusual breed or a dog with special needs, find out if the trainer has experience with dogs like yours.

The best way to find a good class is to locate a local obedience or kennel club through the American Kennel Club or United Kennel Club (see below). If that club doesn't offer classes, they can often refer you to a reputable instructor. If no such classes exist, and if enough people are interested, perhaps a successful exhibitor or trainer can be convinced to offer classes.

## WAGGIN' WORKSHOPS
### *PURSUE HIGHER EDUCATION*
**Abilities:** Varies by class

Maybe you're getting serious about some of the activities you share with your dog. Maybe you wish you could spend the day with a dog authority. Canine experts in behavior, showing, obedience, agility, tracking, swimming, massage—just about anything

## Workshop and Seminar Listings

American Kennel Club: www.akc.org/dic/seminars.cfm

Animal Assisted Therapy: www.create-a-smile.org/upcoming.htm

Association of Pet Dog Trainers: www.apdt.com/events.htm

Canine University: www.canineuniversity.com/seminars.html

Competing: www.competingatyourpeak.com/seminars_
workshops.html

Delta Society: www.deltasociety.org/dsq001.htm

Grooming: www.members.aol.com/groomingschool/
programs1.htm

Legacy Training Seminars: www.legacycanine.com

Puppyworks: www.puppyworks.com

Retriever workshops: www.retrieverguide.com

Search and Rescue: www.sardog.org/trainings.htm

Sled Dogs: www.sleddogcentral.com/seminars.htm

T-Touch: www.tteam-ttouch.com/cgi-bin/webcal.pl

that has to with dogs—often travel to give workshops in many areas. The workshops enable you and your dog to find out the latest in techniques and get one-on-one instruction. Local dog clubs usually sponsor these events. If you have a particular expert in mind, work with a club to bring that expert to town.

## MEET AND GREET
### *MAKE SOME NEW FRIENDS*
**Abilities:** Behave in public

Meet and greets are events in which people with dogs, sometimes of the same breed or background, congregate in a public area, usually to promote dog adoptions or some other noble canine cause. Local parks or pet superstores are often good places to hold meet and greets. Some meet and greets center around a particular breed—often one that has a large group of rescue dogs available for adoption. Others spotlight former shelter animals and promote adoption of currently homeless dogs.

You can have some fun events and some fund-raising events, but the whole affair is low-key and the primary goal is for the public to get to know your dogs. That means your dogs have to be on their best behavior—or you can just say you think it's important for potential owners to understand the breed isn't always perfect! You may wish to have handouts for people who want to know more about your breed, or cards for people interested in contacting a rescue group for a dog just like yours.

You get to do a good deed, your dog gets to be the center of attention—not a bad way to spend the day! And you may come home with an extra dog if you fall in love with a shelter pooch. . . .

## BARK AVENUE
### *PUT ON YOUR RUNNING SHOES*
**Abilities:** Jog

Dog-a-thons, where people walk a certain distance with their dogs as part of an organized event, are popular community activities, often attracting many more participants than comparable dogless-a-thons. Most of these events are fund-raisers for local animal shelters, so shelters are a good place to ask about upcoming events. Find out if you're expected to get pledges and how far you're expected to walk. If you can't find a dog-a-thon in your area, talk to your animal shelter about organizing their own Boston (Terrier) marathon.

## DOG DAY AFTERNOON
### A CANINE CARNIVAL
**Abilities:** Varies

For a kid, few things can match the excitement of the carnival coming to town. But what's comparable for a dog? A canine carnival! There may not be wild rides, but plenty of other events will have your dog wiggling with excitement. The dogs will enjoy things like doggy party games, petting booths, food samples, doggy massage booths, agility obstacles, races, fenced play areas, group hikes and water parks. The people will enjoy the vendor booths, pet photo booths, pet psychics, exhibitions, prize drawings and people food. Many carnivals offer special events just for kids and their dogs.

Even though your dog may not consider it a highlight, he can also get a bath, get microchipped or have his nails clipped. Spectators can enjoy celebrity guests and exhibitions by drill teams, flyball teams, disc catchers, agility whizzes, herding dogs, search and rescue dogs and police dogs. Some events offer short seminars in behavior, first aid, nutrition, massage or grooming. And some offer introductory lessons in obedience, agility, carting, dancing, disc catching or dog showing.

Your dog may be able to earn a Canine Good Citizen title, and you can be a good citizen by helping raise money for homeless animals. Pet adoption booths are a big part of these events, complete with dogs waiting to go home with somebody and lots of information about how to take care of them.

You can also have smaller events for smaller crowds. Arrange a Fur Ball—an elegant affair with dancing, fine food and fundraising. Or howl at the moon with a late evening outing under the stars and around the campfire—just keep the tails out of the fire!

No such events in your area? There should be. In large communities they attract thousands of people and dogs, and raise

> ## Event Listings
>
> Animal Event listings: www.animalevent.com
>
> Great American Mutt Show: www.greatamericanmuttshow.com
>
> The Poop Pet Resources: www.thepoop.com/events/default.asp

thousands of dollars for humane groups. Smaller communities may not be able to offer as many events or attract as large a crowd, but they do a great job of raising money, placing homeless dogs, promoting responsible dog ownership, fostering the human-canine bond and furthering the dog's good image in the community. Perhaps you should start a committee. . . .

## TAKE IN A SHOW

### GO TO A DOG COMPETITION

**Abilities:** Behave in public, varies by event

You don't need to have a fancy show dog to enjoy going to a dog show or other dog competition. In fact, many competitions are open to dogs of any breed or mixture of breeds. Check out Chapter 7, "The Best Organized Sports," to get an idea of what's available for you and your dog. Even conformation shows often hold Canine Good Citizen tests (page 127) that you can enter while you're at the show.

If you're not the competitive type, you and your dog may enjoy attending simply as spectators. Most events have vendors selling every imaginable piece of puppy paraphernalia. Be sure to check out the rules or call ahead before you show up; while some events welcome all dogs, other events don't allow unentered dogs to attend.

Many people attend dog events more for the social opportunities than the competitive aspects. They may travel every weekend, camping out in motor homes or vans in giant campsites devoted to dogs. Many strong friendships are formed. While evenings are often relaxed and filled with leisurely chat, the days are often intense and hectic. Even if you don't have a dog of your own in competition, you can be part of the excitement by volunteering to help hold dogs or do any other essential tasks for which there are never enough helpers. Or you and your dog can just mosey around and relax and watch the show.

## BARK IN THE PARK
### *FIND A DOG PARK*
**Abilities:** Play well with others

*No dogs allowed.* Sometimes it seems those signs are everyplace—or at least everyplace that looks fun. Beaches, picnic areas, playgrounds, parks—they all have gradually turned to banning dogs. At the same time, specialty parks have popped up for kids with bikes, skateboarders and every kind of sport. Yet a huge part of the population has at least one dog in the family. Recently, people have started realizing that dogs deserve their own park, too—a place where they can run loose in safety and not bother anybody who doesn't like dogs. A dog park. The idea has caught on, and dog parks, also called dog runs, are thriving.

Where else can your dog make buddies with a dog from another breed and another home? Where else can he race his friends around a fenced area? You can get in there and play with the dogs, or sit on the sidelines and talk to the other dog lovers.

Some parks are huge, complete with hiking trails. Some are small, but may include playground-like agility equipment. Some have a pond for swimming and retrieving. Many have separate areas for large and small dogs. Most have rules: no aggressive dogs, no unvaccinated dogs, no females in heat and no more than a certain number of dogs per person. They all require that you clean up after your dog. Bring water, a bowl and baggies for waste disposal. Some parks supply these, but it will be just your luck that they've run out the day you need them.

You can't just go to a dog park and throw your dog to the wolves, so to speak. If the area is crowded with boisterous dogs, wait for them to tire out before asking if you can make introductions with your dog. If your dog isn't used to other dogs, ask if they can meet through a fence, or better, by walking alongside one another on a leash.

Unfortunately, lots of people who go to dog parks have no idea about dog behavior. Too many people suffer from the "he just wants to be friends" syndrome, in which their dog pushes himself at your dog, sniffing and staring and generally intimidating yours. "Oh, he just wants to be friends!" they exclaim as your dog cowers and tries to get away. How would you like a stranger coming over and pushing himself on you? Now you're embarrassed, and your dog is labeled antisocial, snobbish or cowardly. She may even snap in self-defense, so she's labeled vicious and perhaps banned from the park. Yet the dog at fault was the bad-mannered dog who thrust himself upon her, and the people at fault were that dog's owner—and you, for not stopping it.

Other dogs may just not get along. Dogs take an instant dislike to some other dogs, and two dominant dogs may be itching for an excuse to fight. One accidental bump, one ball they both get to at the same time, or even one dirty look and you have a dogfight on your hands.

Innocent accidents can have serious repercussions because groups of dogs can exhibit pack behavior. One dog can get hurt or frightened and begin to yelp, another dog will give chase and suddenly every dog in the park is running down the shrieking dog. Such a scenario can be catastrophic. Don't run little dogs with groups of big dogs. And don't allow little children, who could also start crying and running, in the middle of a group of unfamiliar dogs.

The best way to avoid problems is to train your dog to come when called, to socialize her so she's comfortable and well-mannered around other dogs, to learn to read her and other dogs' body language behavior, and to be on the lookout for dogs who could spell trouble. Don't get so preoccupied talking to the other people that you don't watch your dog.

Despite all this, relatively few problems actually occur in dog parks, and the biggest problem most people have with dog parks is dragging their dogs out of them when it's time to go home. That, and you eventually have to learn to spell the word "park," as in "I need to P-A-R-K the car," or your dog will start spinning in circles and you'll have to take him to one.

Check out the dog park websites for parks in your area. If you don't have one, they even have directions on how to start one.

## Dog Park Directories

Dog Park: www.dogpark.com

The Dog Park: www.thedogpark.com

Dog Fun Directory: www.ilovethisplace.com/dogfun/

Urban Hound: www.urbanhound.com

## MUTT STRUT

### *A PARADE OF POOCHES*

**Abilities:** Heel, behave in public

The band plays. The crowd cheers. And you're marching down the middle of Main Street with your dog by your side. Deep down you've always wanted to be in a parade. Now your dog and you can dazzle the crowd as part of a doggy drill team.

Of course, you can't just show up the day of the town parade with some buddies and their dogs and call yourself a drill team (although the comedic aspects might be entertaining). First you have to find some people with similar aspirations. Obedience clubs are a good source. Your dogs don't have to be obedience masterminds, but should be good at heeling and at looking happy while they're doing it.

Then you have to figure out a routine that involves more than milling about aimlessly. Think of how your formations will look from the side and even from overhead (think Macy's Thanksgiving Day Parade). The more people you have, the more complex your basic moves will appear. You can heel in marching formation, weave in and out, go in spirals and circles—use your imagination and see if you can make it happen. Learn your formations without your dogs; this is their chance to lounge and laugh at you and your chance to get your footwork right without stepping on them. Then get your dogs, choose some appropriate music, start practicing and have fun! An easy routine with happy dogs will be more appreciated than a difficult routine with unhappy dogs.

As you progress, you can add props or spotlight the abilities of certain dogs. But never design a routine that makes one dog irreplaceable. Make sure your formations will still work if somebody calls in sick on parade day. Also make sure your routines can be downsized in case you end up in an alley rather than a four-lane highway. Acclimate your dogs to crowds and marching band noises. Then call your local city hall and find out how to get on the roster for your town's next parade.

Actually, you'll find more audiences outside of parades. Schools and nursing homes can be good places to show off and polish your show. And they tend to be appreciative even if you mess up. Start little, aim high, have fun and march on!

## VISITING HOURS

### THERAPIST IN A FUR COAT

**Abilities:** Basic obedience, trustworthiness around people

You know how much better your dog makes you feel when you're down or lonely. Have you ever considered sharing his love with people who have no pets? Maybe it's the shut-in down the street who would relish a visit from a neighbor with a dog. Maybe it's a shelter for abused women and their children. Maybe it's your grandmother in a nursing home—or the rest of the residents there. Maybe it's a long-term care facility for children. Maybe it's your kid's school class, or maybe it's a class for more challenged children. These are all opportunities for you and your dog to make a real difference in people's lives.

Of course, you want that difference to be a good one. Your dog must be immaculately clean, calm and trustworthy around new people and in unusual situations, and sufficiently obedient to refrain from jumping on people. Depending on the situation, your visits may involve simply allowing a person to calmly stroke your dog, encouraging children to play with your dog or giving drill-team or trick demonstrations for groups. Your dog needs to be tolerant of situations in which he may be surrounded by admirers or petted a little too roughly. You need to be adept at graciously removing him from such situations.

Dogs can help children build confidence and give them the desire to push themselves to throw balls and interact. A dog is also

## Therapy Resources

Delta Society: www.deltasociety.org, (425) 226-7357

Therapy Dogs International: www.tdi-dog.org, (973) 252-9800

Therapet: www.therapet.com

Therapy Dogs Inc.: http://therapydogs.com/

Service and Therapy Dogs: www.cofc.edu/~huntc/service.html

Local groups: www.dog-play.com/therapyl.html

The Healing Paw Online Newsletter: www.thehealingpaw.org

Burch, Mary, *Wanted! Animal Volunteers*, Howell Book House, 2002.

Davis, Kathy Diamond, *Therapy Dogs; Training Your Dogs to Help Others*, Dogwise Publishing, 2002.

a great way to get children's attention and open the door for pet care education. Dogs tend to help people open up, and you're sure to be treated to wonderful stories of dogs who live on in people's memories.

Although you can do some of these activities informally, you can also join a group that will prepare you and your dog for the situations you'll encounter. They will arrange visits to various facilities and give you the option of going alone, with a friend or with a group. Your dog can attend a course and, upon passing, become a certified therapy dog.

More formal therapy programs involve more training and professional interaction. Dogs can act as true therapy assistants, helping patients improve physical, cognitive, social and emotional functioning. For example, brushing a dog may improve arm strength and coordination. Telling a dog to perform tricks may improve communication skills. Training a dog may increase self-esteem. Playing with a dog may increase activity levels. These formal programs must be undertaken under the supervision of a professional in that area.

Making the commitment to volunteer with your dog is not something to be taken lightly or purely for your own gratification. People will come to count on you and your dog. You can make a positive difference in someone's life, but if you don't live up to your commitments, or if you handle yourself poorly, or if your dog isn't up to the demands of the job, you can also make a negative difference. Not every dog enjoys visiting strangers, and not every person enjoys or benefits from having a dog come visit. But more often than not you'll find it's one of the most fulfilling things you can do with your dog, and you'll understand why some of the best therapists wear fur coats.

# Chapter 5

# The Best Doggy Vacations

It's not fair. When your friends go on vacation they take their families. When you go on vacation you're expected to leave yours behind in a kennel. How many times have you returned home early from vacations because you felt guilty about your dog? Or just decided not to take a vacation at all? Sure, your dog will be happy to just hang around the house with you and play games, but the two of you really deserve to get out of town.

If you're adventurous, you can go camping in the wilderness where nobody can complain that your campmate is canine. But what if bugs and dirt and prepackaged food aren't your idea of a vacation? You can spin the wheel of chance, plop your dog in the car and just hope you'll end up somewhere your dog is tolerated. But there's a better solution. Plan a vacation where your dog isn't just tolerated, but is welcomed! Plan a *real* family vacation that makes the most of having your canine family member along.

# THE VACATIONS

## ROVING WITH ROVER
### HITTING THE ROAD
**Abilities:** Behave in the car and in public

Some of the best vacations have no destination. They're the ones where you get in your car and drive, and each night you end up somewhere you never knew existed. Dogs love this kind of trip. After all, it's the way they live their lives.

But is taking your dog for a road trip really going to be fun? It can be. A canine copilot can steer you to destinations you might otherwise have passed, give you a good excuse to stop and enjoy the scenery up close and help you have the road trip of a lifetime. But unless you plan ahead, motels, parks, attractions and beaches may turn you away. And be warned: Even the quietest dog will find plenty to bark at once she discovers you're trying to sneak her into a motel room. Several books are available that list establishments that accept pets. Get one.

Keep an eye out for little nature excursions, which are wonderful for refreshing your dog and you. But always do so with a cautious eye; never risk your or your dog's safety by stopping in totally desolate areas, no matter how breathtaking the view. Always walk your dog on a leash when traveling. If she gets frightened or distracted, your dog could become disoriented and lost. Your dog should be wearing a collar with license tags, including a tag indicating where you can be reached while on your trip, or including the address of someone you know will be at home.

Bliss for a dog is a ride in the car with the wind in her fur and bugs in her teeth as she hangs her head out the window and enjoys! Sure, that would be fun while it lasted, but it might not last long before your dog is thrown from the car, gets her nose stung by a bee or gets her eye put out by a rock. Kids would love to run around the car and hang out the windows but there are laws for their safety (and yours) that prevent them from doing so. We won't even talk about the danger involved in letting dogs ride loose in the back of pickups!

Your dog has a higher center of gravity than you do when riding in the car, and far less ability to grab onto something. It doesn't take much to send a dog flying into the dash, windshield, you, or out of the vehicle altogether. Loose dogs have been killed and injured in relatively small accidents. Dogs have also caused accidents by getting a leg caught in the steering wheel, bumping the car out of gear or jumping in the driver's lap at the wrong moment.

You can buckle your dog up with a doggy seatbelt or secure her in a crate that has been securely fastened so it won't go flying. On the crate should be a sticker or tag that reads "In case of an accident: Take this dog to a veterinarian, then contact the following persons (list names and phone numbers), who have guaranteed payment of all expenses incurred." Remember that you may not be able to speak for your dog in the event of a serious accident.

You know better than to leave your dog in the car on a warm day. But what do you do when you have to sprint inside to the rest room? You can use battery-powered fans that run off your cigarette lighter to help circulate air, but they won't cool the car down. You can park in the shade and crack the windows, but you risk escape or dognapping. If you have a crate, you can place your dog in it, padlock the crate door and padlock the crate to the car for security. You can also use one of the cooling pads made for dogs (check out www.malinut.com/write/kool.shtml or www. airsafeusa.com/coolzone/#CVest). *Never* leave your dog tied in or to your car.

In warm weather your dog will save you money by forcing you to bypass all the expensive attractions and stores you may have otherwise visited. Many attractions do, however, have boarding arrangements for pets. Check ahead to find out what facilities are available, or consider day care at a boarding kennel near the attraction.

In some cases, air travel is a better way to get there. If your dog can fit in a traveling crate under the seat, she may be able to ride in the cabin. Larger dogs have to ride in the baggage compartment. Although baggage compartments are heated, they are not air-conditioned, and in hot weather dogs have been known to overheat while the plane was still on the runway. For that reason many airlines don't accept summer shipping. When you make your airline reservations, you must mention that you are flying with a dog.

Buy an airline-approved crate that meets certain specifications for size, strength and ventilation. If your dog is not crate-trained, set the crate up in your house well before your trip and get your dog used to eating and sleeping in it. Ready the crate for the trip by securing its fasteners super tight, adding bedding that can be thrown away at your destination if soiled, and finding a water bowl or bucket that won't spill and that your dog's head can't get caught in. You can hang a bucket from the crate door with an eyebolt snap. Fill the water bowl with ice that will melt en route.

Once at your destination, where will you stay? If you plan to stay with friends, ask beforehand if it will be OK for you to bring your dog. Never show up with a dirty dog—or worse, one with parasites. Bring your dog's own clean blanket or bed, or better yet, a crate. Your dog will appreciate the familiar place to sleep and your friends will breathe sighs of relief. Even though your dog may be accustomed to sleeping on furniture at home, a proper canine guest stays off the furniture when visiting. Do not allow your dog to run helter-skelter through their home. If your hosts have pets of their own, be sure your dog does not chase or fight with them. Walk and walk your dog (and clean up after her) to make sure no accidents occur inside. If they do, clean them immediately and inform your host. Don't leave them any surprises! Changes in water or food, or simply stress, can often result in diarrhea, so be particularly attentive to taking your dog out often.

The number of establishments that accept pets decreases yearly. Please do everything you can to convince motel managers that dogs can be civilized guests. Leave your dog alone in a motel room only if you can afford to have the room refurbished after your dog has redecorated it. The dog's perception is that you have left her in a strange place and forgotten her; she either barks or tries to dig her way out through the doors and windows in an effort to find you, or becomes upset and relieves herself on the carpet. That's one reason having a crate-trained dog (and a crate) makes travel so much better. You can leave her crated in the room, where she will feel secure and can't damage anything. She will probably take a nap and be nice and fresh and ready for an adventure when you return.

You might think packing for your dog would be a cinch—after all, she's already wearing her entire wardrobe! But unlike you, your dog will need almost all of her food packed, as well as a lot of other things you don't want to have to hunt down in an unfamiliar place. Most of all, you need to pack with your dog's health and safety in mind. Place all of your dog's belongings in a separate bag. It makes things easier to locate and keeps your own stuff from being covered with dog stuff. Consider packing:

- medications, especially anti-diarrhea and heartworm preventive
- food and water bowls
- food and dog biscuits
- chewies and toys
- bottled water or water from home
- flea comb and brush
- bug spray or flea spray
- moist towelettes, paper towels, and self-rinse shampoo
- bedding
- short and long leashes
- flashlight for night walks
- plastic baggies or other poop disposal means
- health and rabies certificates
- recent color photo in case your dog somehow gets lost
- crate

## DOGGY DESTINATIONS
### FUN PLACES FOR DOGS TO GO
**Abilities:** Behave in public

Most people who take their dogs along on trips are happy to just have them tag along while they do what they would have done anyway. The places where they stay allow pets, but these places

# Travel Resources

## Websites

www.1clickpethotels.com

www.aaa.com

www.canineauto.com

www.dogfriendly.com

www.doggonefun.com

www.petsonthego.com

www.takeyourpet.com

www.travelpet.com

www.travelpets.com

## Books

American Automobile Association, *Traveling With Your Pet: The AAA Petbook*, American Automobile Association, 2001.

Greyson, F. and Kingsley, C., *The Portable Petswelcome.com: The Complete Guide to Traveling With Your Pet*, Howell Book House, 2001.

Habgood, D. and Habgood, R., *On the Road Again With Man's Best Friend: United States*, Dawbert Press, 2000.

Martin, D., *Great Vacations for You & Your Dog, USA, 2001-02*, Martin Management Books, 2001.

Morgan, E., *Fodor's Road Guide USA: Where to Stay With Your Pet*, Fodors Travel Publications, 2001.

Walters, H., *Take Your Pet Along: 1001 Places to Stay With Your Pet*, M C E, 2001.

## Magazines

*Fido Friendly Magazine*
966 E. Sutton Dr.
Fresno, CA 93720
www.fidofriendly.com

don't cater to them or have anywhere for them to go to have some fun. You and your dog can have a great vacation like that, but for a special occasion you may want to plan a special vacation at a special place.

Many luxury hotels in big cities offer dog-spoiling services such as special dog treats and menus, and even dog walkers if you can't get out of bed. As much as your dog will undoubtedly enjoy staying in the lap of luxury, she'd probably rather stay where she can do a little running and exploring. I'm talking about canine country inns and resorts.

Some establishments have fenced acreage, beach access or dog-friendly hiking trails. If you want to sample both the adventure of nature and the comfort of a resort, consider staying at such a place.

## CANINE CONGREGATIONS
### NATIONAL MEETING PLACES
**Abilities:** Behave in public

Internet mail groups have brought together people with similar interests from around the world, and not surprisingly, many dog-oriented groups flourish in cyberspace. It's not uncommon for you to have Internet dog buddies you've never met. Eventually you all get the same idea: Why don't we get together sometime? Several breed groups have organized annual events that attract hundreds of people and their dogs.

These events are often held at a dog-friendly beach or park in the off-season, or anywhere people and dogs can get together and have fun. As a bonus, they're often held where local people can meet the dogs and get to know the breed.

The larger events include vendor booths stocked with breed-specific goods, organized just-for-fun contests, field trips, seminars, auctions, ice cream socials for dogs and dinners for people. One of the most impressive is the annual autumn event at Dewey Beach, Delaware, which attracts more than 2,500 Greyhounds—most of them ex-racers—to the oceanfront.

Join an Internet group for your breed or dog activity and see if such an event is planned. If none exists, why not organize one yourself?

## Doggy Destinations

### *Backcountry Getaways*

Four Peaks Adirondack Camps
(Lake Placid, New York)
P.O. Box 76
Jay, NY 12941
US: (800) 373-8445
International: (518) 946-7313
www.4peaks.com/ftramp

### *Resorts*

320 Guest Ranch
Gallatin Gateway, MT
(800) 243-0320

Crystal Crag Lodge
Mammoth Lakes, CA
(760) 934-2436
www.mammothweb.com/lodging/crystal

The Cypress Inn
Carmel, CA
(800) 443-7443
www.cypress-inn.com

Greyfire Farm Bed and Breakfast
1240 Jacks Canyon Rd.
Sedona, AZ 86351
(800) 579-2340

Justin Trails Bed & Breakfast Resort
Sparta, WI
(800) 488-4521
www.justintrails.com

If you have a purebred dog, you can also attend your breed's national specialty. These events attract the best competitors in the country, and often include seminars, raffles and performance events. Even if your dog isn't entered, he can have plenty of fun

Lorelei Resort
Treasure Island, FL
(800) 35-GO-DOG
www.loreleiresort.com

Paw House Inn
1376 Clarendon Ave.
West Rutland, VT 05777
(866) 729-4687
www.pawhouseinn.com

Stanford Inn by the Sea
Mendocino, CA
(800) 331-8884
www.stanfordinn.com

Three Buck Inn
Olympic Valley, CA
(877) 596-5200
www.threebuckinn.com

White Gate Court
Islamorada, FL
(800) 645-GATE
www.whitegatecourt.com

### Web Resources

Bed and Breakfasts that accept pets:
www.lanierbb.com/search/amenity.html

Vacation rentals that accept pets: www.petfriendlytravel.com

Hunting destinations: www.birddogsforever.com/birdhunt
www.versatiledogs.com/destinations.html

meeting the other dogs. Contact the national breed club to find out when and where their specialty will be, and if unentered dogs can attend. (To find out the national breed club for your breed, log on to www.akc.org.)

## CANINE CAMPS
### BACK TO NATURE
**Abilities:** Get along with other dogs, various other abilities

Dog camps are like summer camps for you and your dog, where you spend time with other canine and human campers in a rustic setting. While your dog may not learn to do leatherwork or make lanyards, he can still learn many skills and even merit badges. The two of you can join in swimming, hiking, games, contests and even campfire sing-alongs.

Some camps offer introductory and advanced workshops in almost any area of canine competition, including obedience, agility, flyball, tracking—even acting! Where else can your hound try herding or your lap dog try lure coursing? You can also learn to fine-tune your communications skills with your dog, take professional-quality photos of your dog and have an expert show you the art of canine massage. And you can learn to think up plausible stories to tell your relatives about what you did on your summer vacation.

Some camps include special sessions or activities for puppies, some emphasize prepping for particular competitive activities, some include lectures and education and some are more freeform and just emphasize fun, fun, fun. Some have hundreds of campers at a session and some have only a handful. None allow aggressive dogs or females in season.

Camp sessions typically last from a weekend to a week. Some fees include lodging (which can be cabins, dorm style or private rooms), while others expect you to fend for yourself at bedtime. Camps are set by lakes, in woods, on mountains or on college campuses, and cover from a few to a few hundred acres.

Consider more than simply proximity and price when choosing a camp. Different dogs

**Breed Event Sampler**

Greyhounds Reach the Beach:
www.adopt-a-greyhound.org/
dewey

Golden Retrievers at Goldstock:
www.goldstockonline.com

Specialty Shows:
www.akc.org/dic/natspec.cfm

thrive at different camps. Contact prospective camps and ask lots of questions.

## ON TOUR

### *JOIN A TOUR GROUP*

**Abilities:** Behave in public, get along with other dogs

One day as your car's odometer turns over 100,000 miles yet again, you'll look up and see a tour bus filled with people taking it easy as they leave the driving to someone else.

**Canine Tour Groups**

Fresh Pond Travel
344 Boston Post Rd.
Marlboro, MA 01752
(800) 225-4897
www.freshpondtravel.com

Rovin' With Rover
9461 Briar Dr.
Streetsboro, OH 44241
(888) 757-4584
www.rovinwithrover.com

Maybe you love traveling with your dog but would sometimes like to share some of your adventures (and the work) with humans. A lot of people feel the same way, but unfortunately, canine touring is still in its infancy. One travel agency specializes in organizing tours for dogs and people to attend special dog shows around the world, such as the Crufts Show in England. They sometimes even arrange doggy cruises.

You can also get involved in the dog show world and attend dog shows throughout the country, perhaps car-pooling or expense-pooling with a couple of friends. For example, you can get a group of friends together to charter a bus to take you and your dogs to a dog event you'll all enjoy. Many buses will allow dogs as long as that is part of the deal when the bus is chartered. The bus will come with a real bus driver and you and your friends and the dogs can mingle and chat as you travel. If there are only a few of you a big van will work fine, but one of you will have to drive that yourself.

Maybe dog shows are not your thing, but you'd like to check out a hiking area or dog-friendly beach. You and your friends can plan a tour to a new place each month. Once in awhile you may

# Canine Camp Listings

Camp Dances With Dogs (Lebanon, New Jersey)
234 Gabryszewski Rd., St. Johnsville, NY 13452
www.flyingdogpress.com/camp.html

Camp Dogwood (Ingleside, Illinois)
3540 N. Southport Ave. PMB 178, Chicago, IL 60657-1436
(312) 458-9549
www.campdogwood.com

Camp Gone to the Dogs (Stowe or Marlboro, Vermont)
P.O. Box 600, Putney, VT 05346
(802) 387-5673
www.camp-gone-tothe-dogs.com

Camp Jackpot
1144 Reynolds Rd., Cross Junction, VA 22625
www.campjackpot.com

Camp Ruffin' It (Lytton, British Columbia)
Gordon Park PO Box 37002, Vancouver, British Columbia
V5P 4W7, Canada
(604) 439-8450
www.webcrosser.com/campruffinit/main.htm

Camp Winnaribbun (Lake Tahoe, Nevada)
P.O. Box 50300, Reno, NV 89513
(775) 348-8412
www.campw.com

Competitive Edge Sports Camp
Cornwall-on-the-Hudson, NY
(508) 529-3568
www.dogsofcourse.com

Dog Days of Wisconsin Summer Camp
235 S. Greenfield Ave., Waukesah, WI 53186
(800) CAMP-4-DOGS
www.dogcamp.com

The Dog's Camp (Weaverville, North Carolina)
121 Webb Dr., Marshall, NC 28753
www.thedogscamp.com

Dog Scouts of America
5068 Nestel Rd., St. Helen, MI 48656
(989) 389-2000
www.dogscouts.com

Dogskills Adventure (Oxford, Ohio)
4937 Thornhill Ln., Dublin, OH 43017
www.dogskillsadventure.com

Hand-In-Paw Productions
P.O. Box 413, Garrisonville, VA 22463
(540) 659-6868
highintrial@aol.com

Iron Dogs
P.O. Box 17643, Encino, CA 91416
(310) 491-9973 ext. 777-1000
www.iron-dogs.com/index.html

Legacy Canine Behavior & Training
P.O. Box 3909, Sequim, WA 98382
(360) 683-1522
www.legacycanine.com

Ready For Prime Time Dog Performance Camp (Friendsville, PA)
P.O. Box 413, Garrisonville, VA 22463
(540) 659-6868
www.members.aol.com/highintrial/rfpt.html

Pine Meadows Farm Agility Camp
6125 Woodman Rd. SW, South Boardman, MI 49680
(877) 276-6215
www.pinemeadowsfarm.com/dogcamp.htm

Splash Camp
P.O. Box 842, Monroe, CT 06468
(203) 521-0934
www.splashcamp.com

Wiz Kid Dog Camp (Pennsylvania)
4 Brookside Pl., Westport, CT 06880
(203) 226-9556
wizkid@netaxis.com

even leave the dogs at home and check out some neat places, such as the AKC Dog Museum (www.akc.org/love/museum) outside of St. Louis, Missouri.

## BOATING WITH BOWSER

### *SAIL THE SEVEN SEAS*
**Abilities:** Swim, stay

Many dogs enjoy sharing a canoe ride down a peaceful river, taking in the rising sun from a bass boat on a lake, sampling the sea breeze from a sailboat on the Gulf or watching the dolphins play from the deck of a yacht. These dogs usually have people who have made a special effort to give their dog sea legs.

Any seafaring dog must understand that water is not just a sparkly solid surface. He should know how to swim and how to get back into the boat from the water. And even the best swimmer should wear a life vest when boating.

Practice what you would do in an emergency involving a dog overboard. Getting him back into the boat can be tricky, so make sure your first attempts are not so far from land that he (and you!) couldn't swim to safety. If you're strong you can lift him into the boat; in a little boat you can help by pushing down on his head and pulling up on his chest once he has placed his front feet into the boat. If you're in a larger boat, a long-handled fish net can help scoop up a little dog. A harness or a life vest with a lifting handle can help when you're trying to pick up a larger dog.

Teach your dog to ride calmly and to jump in the water only when you tell him to. Hold your dog when you start your engines or blow your boat horn, because the sound could startle him at first. If you're sailing, let the sail out slowly so the dog can get used to its motion and sound. You should also have a way of safely tethering him when the boat is leaning or accelerating, or as you approach a dock he may try to jump onto. Tether him by his life vest, not his neck!

Make some concessions for your dog. Rig walkways with good traction so your dog doesn't slip from one end of the boat to the other. Provide ramps instead of ladders. Make sure the deck isn't hot by providing shade or carpeted areas. Supply a shady rest area. Dogs can get overheated and sunburned. Keep hooks, bait and fuels out of reach. And beware: Dogs get seasick, too. Avoid housing him in the V-berth, where motion is emphasized. Instead, keep him near the boat's center of gravity and let him cuddle in some secure cushions. Ask your veterinarian about medication if seasickness becomes a problem.

Teach your dog to relieve himself on command. Little dogs can use dog litter boxes, but big dogs may need a trip to shore. You can try training a larger dog to use a box of sod or some Astroturf. Otherwise, be prepared for a poop deck.

On long boating excursions, dogs need to get to shore anyway to run off pent-up energy. Not all marinas allow dogs, so check ahead before heading in. Don't allow your dog to jump to the dock without your permission, and keep him on a leash when you're at the dock. In addition to his other ID, have your boat's marina and slip number on your dog's identification.

## Boating Resources

### Excursions

Dog Paddling Adventures
177 Idema Rd.
Markham, Ontario
Canada, L3R 1A9
(416) 992-2216
www.dogpaddlingadventures.com

Pets on the Go (listing of dog-friendly charters and tours):
www.petsonthego.com/transcruischrtr

### Products

Life vest evaluation: www.boatus.com/pets/dogvest.asp

Boat U.S. Pet Store: www.boatus-store.com/petstore

## Lodging and Destinations Abroad

Australia and New Zealand: www.doggyholiday.com

Australia: www.petsplayground.com.au

Canada: www.petfriendly.ca

Europe: www.dogsabroad.com

Europe: www.petfriendly.co.uk

Japan: www.living-with-dogs.com/en/travel

South Africa: travel.iafrica.com/getaways/149425.htm

United Kingdom: www.dogpeople.ltd.uk

United Kingdom: www.paws4travel.co.uk

United Kingdom: www.petfriendlyhotels.com

United Kingdom: www.thecornishcoast.co.uk

International: www.virtualcities.com/ons/0onsadex.htm

### Quarantine Information

Australian Quarantine:
www.affa.gov.au/aqis/homepage/aqishome

Pet Travel Scheme: www.defra.gov.uk/animalh/quarantine/

## INNOCENTS ABROAD
### SNIFFING FOREIGN SOIL

**Abilities:** Travel in a crate for long periods, behave well in public

Unless you're scandalously wealthy, taking your dog for a weekend in Paris is going to be too expensive and too difficult. But if you're planning to spend a month or more overseas, it may be worth looking into taking your dog with you.

Beware of several factors when making your decision:

- Many countries have strict quarantines. Your dog may spend more time in a quarantine kennel than he would having fun with you. Check out the current regulations dealing with vaccinations and quarantines.

- Many cultures are not dog friendly. You may have difficulty finding lodging or taking your dog places.
- Many areas have problems with stray or diseased dogs. Your dog could be in danger from them, or be suspected of being a stray himself if he's not on a leash.
- Many areas have diseases for which your dog is unlikely to have been immunized.
- Some areas may not have veterinary care that meets the standards you're used to.
- Many areas have wildlife that can kill your dog.

On the positive side, many countries really welcome dogs. European countries are often very dog friendly, and will let you take your dog with you on the bus, into restaurants and other places where dogs are not allowed in the United States. The United Kingdom, which is perhaps one of the dog-friendliest countries in the world, is becoming more accessible to foreign dogs than it used to be. The new Pet Travel Scheme makes it easier for dogs to travel to the U.K., but they still must meet stringent requirements.

Several companies specialize in shipping pets. It is often worthwhile to have them arrange shipping to a foreign country, because the paperwork can get complicated.

# Chapter 6

# The Best Outdoor Adventures

The great outdoors is calling: "Here boy! Come on, girl!" Maybe not in so many words, but with the roar of a mountain stream, the scent of a rabbit in the brush or the vista of an endless prairie, it's calling. And you're sitting inside reading a book? Get up! Get going! There's a wolf in your living room disguised as a dog—and he wants to go back to his roots. Let him lead you on a great outdoor adventure. There's going to be plenty of time to read when you get back and he's sound asleep at your side dreaming of the day's events.

## THE ADVENTURES

### GET WET!
#### *SWIMMING LESSONS*
**Abilities:** None

Do you really need to teach a dog how to dog paddle? Not every dog takes to water right off. But with a few swimming lessons, you can be blessed by wet dog shakes and wet dog smell every time you go near water.

Introduce your dog to water at home with a wading pool, filling it higher every day. Unless yours is a very small dog, the pool will never be deep enough for swimming. But at least your dog can learn how refreshing a water wallow is on a hot day.

When it's time to for a real swim, find a place with inviting, calm water and a gradually sloping entry. Some dogs will rush right in, but even so, you should exercise caution and not let your dog take on more than she's ready for. Other dogs will remain hesitant. You can force such a dog into the water and risk ruining her love of it for life, or you can wisely back off and come back prepared to help your dog love the water.

The best way to help a dog overcome fear of water is to have her wear a doggy life vest. Accustom her to it at home, giving her treats just for wearing it. She should also have a harness, which she should wear even when she no longer needs a life vest. This enables you to guide her and even pull her to safety with a long floating line—something else you need.

Prepare yourself, as well. Your dog could panic in deep water and try to climb on top of your head, clawing you and pushing you underwater in the process. You should have shoes you can wear while swimming and your own life vest, and your vest should have an emergency whistle attached where it won't get tangled around your dog's paws.

Bring several toys and even some treats, such as hot dogs, that float. Now walk into the water and start playing with the toys and treats, encouraging your dog to get one foot wet at a time so she can join you and get her rewards. Make it fun! Having another dog who is already a water lover can show your dog that wading is a doggy thing to do.

As she gains confidence, encourage her to walk with you in wading-depth water. Walk parallel to the shore, occasionally playing and going back to dry land. You can start teaching her commands such as "swim along" or "swim to shore" or "swim to me" that will be handy when she starts to go in over her head. For "swim along" just guide her to walk by your side, much as you would teach her to heel, but—unless you plan to go into water ballet—precision isn't necessary. For "swim to shore," give her the

## Water Hazards

Dogs can drown. Strong surf, undertows, rogue waves, waterfalls, rapids, rushing ditch or creek water, thin ice, cold water and ditches or aqueducts with steep sides have been too much for many strong swimming dogs. If it's unsafe for people, it's unsafe for dogs.

Animals in and around water can also pose threats. Sharks, jellyfish and the Portuguese man-of-war can be a concern in salt water. Sharks are particularly dangerous in areas that have a lot of shark bait, such as fish schools or seals.

Snakes, turtles and alligators can be threats in fresh water. The cottonmouth snake lives in just about any fresh water body in the Southeast. It often basks on the shore during the day, but is more active at night. The aggressive snapping turtle, which is found all over the Eastern and Midwestern states in muddy-bottomed fresh water, can inflict serious bites. The alligator, which lives in fresh or brackish water in the Gulf and coastal Southeastern Atlantic region, loves to eat dogs.

Dogs love to eat dead fish (or at least, roll in them!). Don't let them do either. In the Northwest, raw salmon, steelhead, trout and some other fish are infected with small flukes that contain *Neorickettsia helminthoeca*. Eating infected fish can cause a potentially fatal disorder called salmon poisoning. Rolling in any fish can also cause a potentially serious accident when you try to drive home with your head out the window.

command, then start racing to shore, taking care not to leave her so far behind that she feels deserted or scared. For "swim to me," have a helper hold her on shore or elsewhere in the water, then call her to "swim to me" as your helper releases her. Encourage her as you would if you were teaching her to come, and be sure to give her a treat when she gets to you.

Only when she's wagging and wading along should you encourage her out far enough that her feet no longer touch bottom. If she's wearing her life vest this should not be traumatic. Still, most dogs think they can walk on water and their first swimming efforts are poor because they are trying to lift their front feet above the surface. You can help by holding her rear end up and preventing her front feet from splashing. Even without your help, most dogs will catch on. As she gains confidence, remove her life vest and repeat the process. Stay near shore. If your dog doesn't like the sensation of being in over her head, go back to shallow water and work more slowly.

Give swimming a try, but it's no disgrace to have a Labrador landlubber. Not every dog likes to swim. Many dogs aren't built for it. Different dogs have different levels of buoyancy, according to their body fat, lung capacity and general build. Bulldog-type breeds may not be able to swim at all. Dogs with heavy coats that sop up water may tend to sink.

Swimming is never something you send your dog to do to prove a point or to show the depths of your dog's devotion to you. Never push your dog to do something she doesn't want to do, encourage her to swim when she's tired or place her in a risky situation. Your dog should only go swimming when an adult is present. If you have a pool, have your dog practice getting out by using the steps. Even if your dog hates to swim, she needs to know how to get out of a pool in case she falls in.

Give your dog plenty to drink before taking her swimming. Otherwise she's apt to drink swimming water, which may have a high salt, chlorine or bacteria level.

Don't expect your dog to retrieve while swimming yet. She needs to concentrate on one thing at a time. You can throw items in shallow water so she learns how to scoop them out while they're floating. Only when she gets more confident in the water should you introduce short swimming retrieves. Later, encourage her to rush into the water.

For dogs who love swimming, there's more than just splashing and dog paddling. You can teach your dog to retrieve underwater, sniff out underwater scents, act as a courier, bring you a life vest from shore, tow a boat, tow you to shore, save a life or dive off a dock.

For example, to retrieve underwater, start by throwing your dog's favorite toy into a wading pool where the water is so shallow that less than half the object is submerged. You can use food if your dog isn't motivated by toys. Your goal here is to entice your dog to eventually submerge his nose, then muzzle, then eyes, then whole head—and for most dogs to do this, they're

## Don't Drink the Water!

When your dog drinks seemingly pristine water straight from nature she may ingest *Giardia* and get sick with stomach cramps and diarrhea. *Giardia* is a microscopic organism found in many water sources. It is nicknamed "beaver fever" because of its special propensity to be carried by beavers.

Water doesn't have to be from the wilds to carry microscopic dangers. Pollution, especially in agricultural, industrial or even residential areas, is a much too common threat. Avoid any water that has a peculiar odor, color or surface oiliness, or that is obviously fed by run-off from polluted areas.

going to need all the encouragement they can get. During this process your dog will learn to exhale and blow bubbles through his nose to keep the water out, and to open his eyes so he can still see.

Never force your dog's head under water. I'm sure you realize this will not teach him to be secure around you and water! Gradually work out to greater depths, but realize that not every dog is comfortable retrieving underwater. You may need to stick with items that float, or skip the retrieving entirely. Some dogs, however, will enjoy the game so much that, given clear water, they will dive off a dock and swim underwater to the bottom to retrieve an object.

To teach your dog to tow a boat, start by giving your dog a short floating rope or boat line to hold in his mouth. Throw it for him and have him retrieve it to shore. When he's doing that reliably, have him sit and stay on shore while you place the line in the water, then send him out to retrieve it. You may even attach a little goody package to it so when he brings it back, you open it up and give him the treats! As he gets more proficient, you can increase the length of the line and attach a small floating object. As you increase the size of the floating object, you may wish to accompany him as he swims with it to shore. Eventually you may even be able to get on it and encourage him along. And eventually you can attach the line to a small boat. Be sure you never let him get tired when practicing this; depending on his size and the boat's size, you may wish to only have him tow it a few feet. Keep it safe and keep it fun!

To teach your dog to dive off a dock, start on shore. There's a secret to getting a dog to dive off the end of a dock and sail through the air. As with all dog training, you start easy, by encouraging your dog to jump for a toy, first on dry land and then in shallow water. Then leave the dog on shore—either have somebody hold him or teach him to wait—and encourage him to run to you to jump up and catch the toy. Next throw the toy a teeny bit away from him as he begins to jump so he has to stretch his jump a little bit to catch it. Only when he's doing this zealously do you move to a very low dock.

Before encouraging your dog to dive off a dock or bank, check for underwater hazards that could injure, or even impale, a diving dog. With the dog at the end of the dock, throw the toy over the water so he can jump up and catch it and land in the water. His first dock dive! Gradually move him farther back on the dock so he has to run to leap for the toy. Then gradually throw the toy farther out so he has to lengthen his jump. Eventually he won't be able to catch it, but by then he'll be having so much fun flying, it won't matter.

**Water Dog Resources**

Canine Water Sports: www.caninewatersports.com

Wet Dog: www.wetdog.com

## SEE SPOT RUN
### *JOGGING*
**Abilities:** Heel

Need to get in shape? Wish you had a coach to goad you off the couch? You probably do, and he'll be glad to pant with you wherever you go. Dogs can make good running partners, but not all dogs are marathon material. Some dogs, such as tiny dogs or stocky dogs, may not be built for distance running. Old or ill dogs may not be able to do what they once could. Puppies shouldn't

### Hot Dogs

Follow the 120 rule. When the temperature plus the humidity level adds up to 120 or more, avoid strenuous exercise for your dog. Dogs don't have as efficient a cooling system as humans. One of the top causes of summertime canine deaths is jogging or running beside a bicycle until the dog collapses from heat prostration. When this emergency occurs, you probably won't be close enough to a water source with which to thoroughly wet the dog, nor close enough to a car to rush the dog to an animal hospital for help. You do your dog no favors by running him in the heat.

be pushed to do what they eventually will be able to. Other dogs will need to work up gradually to condition their muscles, cardiovascular system and footpads. Most dogs will try to push themselves beyond the point they should—after all, they're running with their best friend! So you need to be the smart one.

Pay special attention to your dog's pads, especially when running on pavement. Coating them with a pad toughening salve may help a little. Hot pavement can be especially damaging. So can hot weather, so don't go jogging without water for you and your running buddy.

Consider forming a neighborhood jogging group of people and dogs. If you're up for bigger challenges, find a dog-a-thon and join other dog and people teams in a long-distance run.

## SPINNING YOUR WHEELS
### BIKING
**Abilities:** Heel, stop

Just about anybody who has a dog and a bicycle eventually looks at both of them and starts thinking, "Hmmm . . . I wonder . . ." Before too long they're pedaling down the drive with the dog eagerly trotting alongside. Everything is right with the world. Then the neighbor's cat runs across the street. . . .

## Home, James

Not every dog can run the Tour de France, or even the Tour de Neighborhood. Consider taking your less athletic dog along by towing him in a bicycle trailer. You can get one especially made for dogs (such as the Pet-A-Lon, from Hammacher Schlemmer; 800-543-3366; www.hammacher.com), or you can modify a utility or child trailer made for bicycles. A good dog trailer should be comfortable, lightweight, difficult to tip over and have a way to prevent the dog from jumping out. Shade is a deluxe touch!

A good percentage of people who think it would be great to bike with their dog end up with lots of bandages on them. Biking with your dog can be fun, but only if you prepare a little. Your dog should know how to heel on a leash and should be in approximately the heel position as you ride. She should know some basic commands, especially "stop!" If she cannot be controlled around cats and squirrels, she should not go biking. Don't tempt her, though—avoid biking through areas with wild animals and loose dogs.

Get her used to the bike by walking her alongside it and then riding very slowly. It's tempting to hold her by looping her lead around the handlebars. Don't! You will experience a dramatic change of direction when your dog forges ahead or stops—so dramatic that you tend to fly off the bike. Holding the dog's leash in one hand is better, but has the drawback that the dog can still upset the bike, and upset you when she pulls you off the bike. In an emergency you can drop the leash, but in an emergency should you really be letting your dog go? No.

The best solution is something designed just for biking dogs called a Springer (see www.dog-training.com/springer.htm). It's a flexible spring-like arm that attaches to the bike's frame and holds the dog out to one side, acting as a shock absorber and preventing the dog from sticking her nose in the wheel spokes.

## TAKE A HIKE
### HIKING
**Abilities:** Heel, carry a backpack

No doubt the healthiest activity you can share with your dog is walking. Whether your hike is around the neighborhood or along the Appalachian Trail, it's also one of the most enjoyable. You don't have to be an expert to be good at walking a dog, but you do need a little good sense.

If you prefer city hiking, be sure you have a safe walking area well off the roadway. Be prepared for stray dogs who can start fights or chase you and your dog into the streets. It's a good idea to carry some sort of dog deterrent, such as the mild pepper spray that letter carriers carry (available in many cycling stores). You can also carry a soda can filled with pebbles that makes a startling noise when you shake it, which is often enough to dissuade an unfamiliar dog.

If you use a retractable leash, don't let your dog run into the road (where he can get hit by a car) or into people's yards (where he can water and fertilize their lawns). Make sure you check your dog's feet, clean up after him, don't walk in dark alleys and leave a trail of bread crumbs so you can find your way home. Other than that, city walking is pretty simple.

Trail hiking is another matter. You need to bring supplies, be prepared for emergencies and above all, know the dangers of the area in which you're hiking. You also need to plan according to your dog's and your own physical limitations. Be sure you head back for home or camp well before either of you even begins to get tired, and well before weather or lighting conditions change the nature of your hike. Consider what you would do if your dog became injured and couldn't walk. Could you carry him back? Could you get help? Remember that the biggest danger is probably evil people you meet in the wilderness. Don't make yourself vulnerable simply in search of the path less traveled.

For a day hike, consider taking the following:

- water with a collapsible bowl
- cellular phone

- small first-aid kit
- leather or nylon leash
- retractable long leash
- collar with tags bearing a local address and phone number; you can have instant tags made at many pet supply stores if you're hiking out of your local area
- harness (handy for helping your dog through rushing water, over slippery ice or up an embankment)
- dog booties (helpful for protecting paws from snow, rocks and briars, and for protecting any cut paws your dog may get on the trail)
- laminated card with your veterinarian's number and permission to treat your dog
- loud whistle
- baggies for waste disposal

If that sounds like a lot of stuff, you may be able to get your dog to carry his own weight (or at least some of it) by fitting him with a backpack. A dog in good condition can carry up to one-third his own body weight, although this will vary according to his build. He will also need to work up to this weight, practicing jumping and climbing with lighter-weight packs first.

Get a nonrestrictive pack that has a V-shape rather than horizontal strap across the front, because the horizontal strap impedes forward movement of the front legs. Padded packs are good for heavy loads, bony bodies or short coats. The ideal pack is made of lightweight waterproof material and has adjustable straps and quick-snap buckles. High visibility orange will help protect your dog from hunters and help you find him if you become separated.

Distribute the weight of items in the pack evenly. Any weight your dog carries should be centered over his shoulder blades, which have the strongest support, rather than over the middle of his back, which is weaker. Anything that goes in the dog's backpack should be secured in waterproof plastic bags, and even so, you shouldn't put anything in there that can't withstand an unscheduled swim.

Don't hike blind. Study a map of your proposed trail and make sure it doesn't contain features that are dangerous or difficult for dogs, such as rope bridges or sheer cliffs with people-size foot-holds. Your hiking boots may save your feet from sharp glass, rocks and burrs, but unless your dog is used to wearing dog boots, you need to consider another route.

Although the idea of letting your dog frolic around you off-leash on the trail is appealing, it's also dangerous for your dog and rude to other hikers. Bring a retractable leash for open areas and a short, sturdy leash for narrow trails.

The best place for your dog is just behind you. If she hikes in front of you, she can trip you and she will also tend to encounter danger before you know it's there. If she walks beside you you'll find yourself fighting over trail space in narrow passages. Use a hiking stick to bar her forward progress, saying "place," and she'll soon learn that walking behind you is the correct place for trail walks.

Keep your dog close and well-mannered when passing other hikers. Remember, many people are uneasy around dogs, and unfamiliar dogs may not get along well. Horses and pack animals may bolt if your dog threatens them. Don't allow your dog to harass wildlife. Besides, some wildlife may fight back.

## Hiking Gear

Outdoor Gear
(877) 288-2008
www.youractivepet.com

Trailhound Gear Shop
(866) DOG-PACK
www.trailhound.com

Fido Gear
(877) FIDO-GEAR
www.fidogear.com

Ruff Wear
(888) RuffWear
www.ruffwear.com

Wolf Packs
(541) 482-7669
http://wolfpacks.com/

Unless you're near safe water for your dog to cool off in, it's best not to hike in warm weather. In moderately warm weather bring a spritzer bottle filled with ice water that you can spray on your dog.

Don't let your dog destroy nature, wildlife or any vacation spot. Don't take stupid chances. Even if your dog is street-smart and obedient at home, you never know what could happen when your dog is in unfamiliar territory. Dogs have run away in fright

## Hiking Destinations

USDA National Forests: www.fs.fed.us

National Parks: www.nps.gov

Bureau of Land Management Lands: www.blm.gov

Recreation on Public Lands: www.recreation.gov

Pet Friendly Activity Guides: www.travelpet.com

Hiking Trails Index: www.hikingwebsite.com/trails/index.htm

Dog Beaches: www.tidalflats.com/Dog_Beaches.html

Dog Beaches: www.totalescape.com/active/animals/dogs/beaches.html

Trail Maps and Descriptions: www.hiker.org

Hike With Your Dog: www.hikewithyourdog.com

Peak to Peak Trail and Wilderness Links: www.peaktopeak.net

GORP Guides to Dog-Friendly Hikes: www.gorp.com/gorp/eclectic/pets.htm

Dog Infomat: www.doginfomat.com/dogparks.htm

Appalachian Trail:
www.appalachiantrail.org/hike/hike_info/dogs.html

Explorer Dog Hikes in Western Washington:
www.explorerdog.com/hikes/

Dog Friendly Hikes near Baltimore:
www.geocities.com/Yosemite/Trails/5434/

Salt Lake, Utah, District: www.fs.fed.us/wcnf/slrd/dogs.html

from pounding surf, strange sights, overwhelming tourists or other loose dogs. They can become intoxicated with the excitement of the woods or beach. Once on the run, they can become easily lost. They can give chase to wild animals that can lead them into the path of traffic. They can wander into agricultural country and be shot by suspicious farmers or ranchers, or into the wilds and be shot by trigger-happy hunters. Are you convinced that your dog is better off hiking on a leash?

Check ahead to make sure you aren't making a trip for nothing. Most public lands allow dogs only on leash or not at all. Most, but not all, national forests allow dogs on trails. But dogs are not allowed on national park or national monument trails. State parks and forests vary in their dog rules. Bureau of Land Management lands allow dogs, but tend to be remote and often have lots of wildlife.

## Hiking Hazards

**Mountain lookouts.** Many dogs have no fear of heights and will teeter along the brink of the Grand Canyon without concern. Dog paws lack the grasping ability of human hands, and once dogs begin to slip they can do little to stop themselves. Snow can cover hidden ravines and cliff edges. Mountain and foothill areas may also be home to abandoned mine shafts and their air vents.

High altitudes can be a problem for older dogs, dogs with heart or lung problems or some brachycephalic (short-nose) breeds. The higher the altitude, the less available oxygen, and unless your dog's body is acclimated she can get shortness of breath or altitude sickness. Hikers setting out from low altitudes on a hot day may find themselves unprepared for the cold temperature when they finally reach the peak.

The mountains are home to many wildlife species, most of which will try to avoid you and your dog. Deer, bighorn sheep, elk and mountain goats will usually run from dogs, posing a potential danger to dogs giving chase along precarious mountainsides. Grizzly bears may or may not try to avoid a confrontation.

**Desert dangers.** The desert is unforgiving. Bring plenty of water even if you have no intention of getting out of your car.

Most desert and chaparral animals are reclusive. Tarantulas, scorpions and Gila monsters are primarily nocturnal and hide in crevices by day. The pig-like javalina is a tough customer who travels in groups in the Southwestern plains and foothills. They can rip a dog from shoulder to hip in a single swipe of their sharp tusks. Coyotes and coydogs generally avoid people and pets, but in some parts civilization has encroached to such an extent that they roam suburbs and campgrounds. Keep small dogs protected at night when in coyote country.

## Hiking and Camping Resources

### E-mail Groups

Canine Backpackers: www.groups.yahoo.com/group/caninebackpackers/

Traildog: www.groups.yahoo.com/group/Traildog/

### Canine Hiking Groups

California Canine Hikers
2154 Woodlyn Rd., Pasadena, CA 91104
http://home.pacbell.net/acanfiel/

Canine Hiking Club of Arizona
www.mydogateaz.com/k9hike.html

Chester County (Pennsylvania) Canine Hiking Club:
http://home.mindspring.com/~miriamhughes/

Dog Hikers of Georgia
270 South Atlanta St., Roswell, GA 30075
(770) 992-2002

K-9 Committee, Angeles Sierra Club
4055 Madison Ave., Culver City, CA 90232
www.angeleschapter.org/k9

K9 Trailblazers (DC/Baltimore, MD): www.k9trailblazers.org

Northern Arizona Canine Hikers
P.O. Box 51014, Parks, AZ 86018

Sierra Club
85 Second St., 2nd Floor, San Francisco, CA 94105
(415) 977-5500
www.sierraclub.org

Much of the desert plant life is cactus, the most infamous of which is the cholla jumping cactus of the Sonoran Desert region. Its thorns seem to jump into a victim's flesh at the slightest brush.

**Woodland warnings.** Woodland wildlife can be a problem if your dog decides to give chase. A fast dog can chase a deer for miles, across roads and into unknown lands. Or chase a skunk only far enough to get a free sample or its aromatic defense.

Tahoe Trail Trekkers
(530) 546-3452

Waggin' Trail Adventures
69 Greyabbey Trail, Scarborough, ON M1E 1V8
(416) 700-5987
www.waggintrailadventures.freeservers.com

### More Information

Camping With Your Dog: www.coyotecom.com/dogcamp.html

Dog Packing Guide: www.wolfpacks.com/guide.htm

Dog First Aid Kit: www.golden-retriever.com/firstaid.html

Best Dog Hikes in and Around Los Angeles: www.spotted
dogpress.com/dog.htm

### Books

Acker, R., *Field Guide: Dog First Aid Emergency Care for the
Hunting, Working, and Outdoor Dog*, Wilderness Adventures Press,
1994.

Hirsch, C., *Canine Colorado: Where to Go and What to Do with
Your Dog*, Fulcrum, 2001.

LaBelle, C., *Guide to Backpacking With Your Dog*, Alpine, 1992.

Mullally, L., *Hiking With Dogs*, Falcon Publishing Company, 1999.

Richmond, R. and Barash, M., *Ruffing It: The Complete Guide to
Camping With Dogs*, Alpine, 1998.

Equally dreaded is the porcupine. These walking pincushions can't "shoot" their quills, so most dogs oblige them by getting close enough for the porcupine to embed a muzzle full of quills with a slap of the tail. Aside from being quite painful and potentially blinding, the barbed quills continue to work their way ever deeper into the flesh with every movement. The best way to remove them is with a quick jerk with a pair of pliers, an essential tool in porcupine country. Black bears, raccoons, wolverines and fishers would rather avoid a dog, but can more than hold their own when pushed.

The rich assortment of mammal life makes the woodlands popular for trapping and hunting. In northern woodlands dogs can be tempted by bait set to entice fur species. Ditches are a favorite site for traps. Know your trapping and hunting seasons and know your hunting areas. Even when you're running your dog off-season in a No Hunting area, don't forget about poachers. Have your dog wear a bright hunter's orange vest—many types and styles are available for hunting dogs.

**Prairie perils.** The prairies share many of the animals of the woodlands and mountains, including deer, jackrabbits and skunk, while adding bison, wild horses, pronghorn antelope and badgers. Most dogs aren't dumb enough to attack a bison or a wild horse, but they can chase pronghorn far away.

Perhaps the most commonly encountered grassland danger is the innocuous looking foxtail. The foxtail is a perennial weedy grass found in fields and on roadsides. It is slender-stemmed with long, bushy flower spikes containing seeds (awns) that embed themselves in dog flesh, most commonly entering the webbing between the toes. Each seed head bears small barbs that point backward, enabling them to travel ever deeper into the body, causing local irritation, infection and even organ failure.

**Here, there and everywhere.** If you're in the South and see abnormally large anthills, keep away! Fire ants range from coastal South Carolina to Texas. They're aggressive and actually inject a tiny amount of venom into any animal that encroaches upon their nest. Their stings hurt and a small dog with lots of stings can die. Other stinging insects, such as hornets, wasps, bees and yellowjackets are a common summer concern nationwide.

Rattlesnakes range over most of the United States. The preferred habitats vary widely among species, but most prefer drier areas, often retreating in burrows, dense vegetation, hollow logs or rock outcroppings. Rattlesnakes make a characteristic rattling sound as a warning, but unfortunately, few dogs are warned off by it.

The copperhead snake's bite is the least toxic of the North American pit vipers, but perhaps the most freely given. Although painful, they seldom are life threatening in a good-sized dog. For small dogs, however, a copperhead bite is an emergency.

Your dog should always be current in his rabies vaccinations before embarking on a hiking trip. Not only do some state parks and all U.S. borders require proof of immunization, but you risk coming across a rabid raccoon, fox or other animal that could infect your pet.

Your dog needs to be on heartworm preventive if you plan to travel in almost any part of the U.S. in summer months, and south Georgia, Florida and the Gulf states in the winter months as well.

## MAPPING A COURSE
### ORIENTEERING
**Abilities:** None

Following a trail is one thing. Blazing your own trail is another, maybe better thing. Orienteering combines cross-country hiking with map and compass reading. The object is to find your way to a series of destinations indicated on a map, choosing the fastest route and getting to the finish in the shortest time.

Orienteering with your dog follows the same basic guidelines as orienteering by yourself, except that it's more fun. Each place to be visited (called a control site) has a marker flag and a way to prove you were there. Although you can use any highly detailed map, the best maps are special orienteering maps that use a special orienteering legend and include magnetic north compass lines. Clues are also often provided. The route between control sites is chosen by the person and dog team. Using a staggered start between teams gives them all a chance to choose their own course. Depending on the experience and physical abilities of the entrants, courses can be from one mile to 20 miles long.

Water is available at each control site. As an added incentive for the dogs, each control site also has a doggy treat stash within 50 feet of it that your dog needs to sniff out. A scent trail may lead to it from the control flag. Each dog finding the stash gets to eat one of the treats. No fair eating them all!

For advanced canine orienteering, every other control site has a scent trail leading to the next site, so the handler is completely dependent on the dog for half the course. If the dog gets lost, clues are provided so the handler can follow a roundabout course and still find the control site.

Many areas have orienteering clubs. It's a good idea to join one to learn the basics first.

## PITCH A TENT

### CAMPING WITH CANINES

**Abilities:** Behave well in public

Imagine falling asleep with the stars as your night-lights, the crickets singing you a lullaby and your dog keeping the chill off. Whether it's in an alpine meadow, a fancy campground or your own backyard, your dog will find camping a great adventure. You'll enjoy it a lot more if you come prepared.

If you're using a tent, set up your tent in your backyard and have a practice camp-out first. This lets your dog realize that the tent is her home no matter where it is. In fact, your dog will probably get just as big a kick from a backyard camp-out as she would from a big outing. It also lets you realize what you've forgotten, and lets you just go inside your house if you decide you weren't cut out for outdoor life.

Start your camp kit with all the supplies listed for a day hike (page 99), plus all the items you would take for a camping trip without a dog, plus:

- a tether or some way to secure your dog's leash to a tree or the ground
- dog bedding and a plastic sheet to place beneath it to keep it dry
- cold protection, such as a dog coat or blanket; it's better than having to share your own clothes with your dog on a cold night!
- dog food stored in an animal-proof container
- dog towel
- insect repellant

If your idea of roughing it is to pull into a campground in your motor home, you'll have lots of room to take your dog's favorite things from home. You'll still want most of the things you would bring for tent camping, plus you can bring a few larger items. The handiest item is an exercise pen so your dog can have her own little yard wherever you camp. It's much safer and easier than tethering.

| Command | Action |
|---|---|
| line out | tighten the towline |
| hike | move forward |
| whoa | stop |
| easy | slow down |
| straight ahead | go straight |
| gee | turn right |
| gee over | move to the right |
| haw | turn left |
| haw over | move to the left |
| on by | pass others without slowing |
| come around | turn around |

## Have Some Pull

### Canicross

**Abilities:** Knowledge of pulling commands

Having a hard time keeping up with your dog on the trail? No wonder—he's got twice as many legs doing the walking as you do! Why not harness his four legs and add them to your two? Hook yourself up to your dog and let him tow you along. This is what's known as canicross—cross country running or walking with your dog.

Canicross is not simply walking the dog—the dog wears a harness and pulls you by a special belt using a line with an integrated shock cord. Your hands are free because your dog is attached at the belt.

Once you're both attached to each other, encourage him to pull by saying "hike!" and having a friend or another dog run in front for him to chase. Of course, you will have to run too. As you approach a right turn, say "gee" (for right); as you want him to turn left, say "haw." This works best on a narrow trail where he can't go any other way. When you want him to stop, say "whoa" and stop.

Canicross is a great way to train for other pulling activities. It's also good for hiking when your dog is tougher than you are. Not only do you get the added power from your dog, but it leaves your hands free. Finally, it's a great way to cheat at dog and human marathons, since your dog can tow you along while everybody else's dog just runs along on a regular leash.

## GET ROLLING
### *ROLLERBLADING*
**Abilities:** Knowledge of pulling commands

Rollerblading with a dog is not as good an idea as it may seem. Compared to biking, you have even less control when it comes to stopping your dog, and most rollerblading is done in fairly populated areas. It's not like you can go trail-rollerblading! If you must live life on the edge, at least make sure you are a skilled rollerblader, that you wear protective gear, that your dog knows the pulling commands and that you don't endanger others as you fly by like an out-of-control rocket should things go wrong.

## SCOOT!
### *SCOOTERING*
**Abilities:** Knowledge of pulling commands

Everybody has a scooter these days. But if you really want to scoot on your scooter, hook up your dog, Skeeter, and get going! The concepts are similar to those used in bikejoring. There's even a book about it, appropriately titled *My Dog Likes to Run; I Like to Ride. How to Train Your Dog To Pull You On a Scooter on City Sidewalks and Country Paths* by Daphne Lewis (DaphneWorks, 1997).

## A BICYCLE BUILT FOR TWO
### *BIKEJORING*
**Abilities:** Knowledge of pulling commands

Do you have the urge to hike but no time? The urge to bike but no power? How about bikejoring? Bikejoring lets you take to the trails on your bicycle, aided by dog power. Of course, there's more to it than simply tying your dog to your bicycle and pedaling away.

If you're buying a mountain bike just for bikejoring, get a sturdy one with front-suspension supports, V-brakes and wide rims. The way you attach your dog to your bike is very impor-tant. The dog must be attached to the middle of the bike so he pulls it straight forward. You have two choices for attachment points: the middle of your handlebars and the stem below them that comes up from the frame. The higher position, on the handlebars, keeps the line from dragging on the front wheel and also steers along with your dog, but is a little less stable because of the higher center of gravity. The lower position is more stable but tends to wear down the line. Try both and see which you find more comfortable. Use the same line and harness you would use for skijoring (see below).

Don't get carried away by being able to ride your bike as fast as you always wanted to. You still have to stop, and you may end up doing that a lot faster than you care to. Wear protective gear and don't run over your dog! If you have more than one dog you can eventually hook up two, or even three, dogs if you are power crazy.

## PULL A FAST ONE

### *SKIJORING*

**Abilities:** Knowledge of pulling commands

If you've ever brought your dog along when you've gone cross-country skiing, you probably figured out pretty fast that it's a good way to cause an accident. You probably also wondered about harnessing some of that dog power to help you on your way home. The sport of skijoring does just that.

Place a comfortable pulling harness on your dog, attach the other end to a specially designed belt on you, and voilà! You have a one-dog power drive unit. The strength of that dog power will vary, of course, depending on your dog. Chihuahuas are not good skijoring dogs. But even a midsize dog can do an admirable job as long as he's in good condition (and by that I mean he's been doing real conditioning exercises). You will need to ski well enough that you don't topple over every few seconds, and you'll need to train your dog on dry land before trying this activity on skis.

Please do not use any old belt and any old piece of rope for skijoring. Get the right equipment (see the box on page 113) and you and your dog will both be safe. Hook your dog's harness to your belt with a bungee cord attached between you and the towline, to lessen the jolt on your dog when he pulls. Practice unhitching yourself from the towline quickly in case of emergency. Teach your dog the commands (see page 109) without skis or snow at first.

As your dog gains experience, you can use a bicycle or cart to continue training (see pages 110 and 116 for these activities).

Avoid hard surfaces, especially asphalt, which can be tough on joints and footpads. Keep it slow and never let your dog get overheated or overworked. As with any dog sport, it's crucial to stop when he still wants more.

If you start in the spring, by the time the snow falls your dog should have the basics down and be ready to try skijoring! Now you will have less control over your dog; you may not be able to stop in shallow snow or ice, and if you hit a bare spot you may stop faster than you'd like. It's critical you learn to slow or stop yourself so you don't ever run into your dog. Just in case, don't use metal-edged skis. For your own safety, wear a helmet and goggles. For the safety of both of you, don't go on frozen ice unless you know it's frozen solid, and avoid trails with motorized traffic.

Icy, crunchy snow will cut canine footpads; keep an eye out for red footprints. If your dog has problems with ice balls accumulating on her feet, spray them with cooking oil. If that does not work, your dog may need to wear snow booties.

After you've endlessly toured all the scenic routes in your own area, consider joining a group for a skijoring trip or taking a skijoring vacation.

## THE DRIVEN SNOW
### SLEDDING
**Abilities:** Knowledge of pulling commands

It's no secret that dog sledding is about the toughest, most time-consuming, most expensive and most addictive of any dog activity. So what's stopping you?

First you'll need sled dogs. Don't be dismayed if your dog isn't a bonafide Husky-type. Dalmatians, German Shorthaired Pointers, Border Collies, Poodles and a bevy of other breeds have made it onto mushing teams. Most good mushing dogs weigh between 40 and 60 pounds and have the urge to pull. You can work with your own dogs and have loads of fun, but if you're serious about getting a top team together, start with dogs from top mushing lines.

Before selling your house and using the money to move the family to Alaska and to buy a team, try it locally with just a few dogs. If you have one dog or two or three, you've got the makings of a good short-distance team, depending on what you want them to pull.

## Skijoring Resources

### Destinations

Alaskan Skijoring Adventures: www.alaska.net/~pattyc/skijor.htm

Arizona Sled Dog Inn: www.sleddoginn.com

Crystal Wood Lodge: www.crystalwoodlodge.com

Telemark Inn: www.telemarkinn.com

TrailsView Treks: www.trailsview.com

Voyageur and Klondike Adventures: www.voyageurventures.ca

Training Trails List: www.sleddogcentral.com/training_trails.htm

XC Ski Areas Directory:
www.xcski.org/xc_directory/xc_skiing_dog.shtml

Boundary Waters Canoe Area, Minnesota, Trails:
www.bwca.cc/activities/skiing/skilodging.htm

### Supplies

Chinook Wind Outfitters: (866) 626-1099;
www.chinookwind.com/skisled.htm

### Book

Hoe-Raitto, M., and Kaynor, C. *Skijor With Your Dog*, OK
Publications, 1992.

### More Information

International Sled Dog Racing Association: (218) 765-4297;
www.isdra.org

North American Skijoring and Ski Pulk Association:
(907) 349-WOOF; www.ptialaska.net/~skijor

Skijor: www.skijor.org/skijor.htm

Skijor Now: www.skijornow.com

Skijorama: www.skijorama.com

Skijoring: www.skijoring.com

A kick sled is a lightweight transportable brakeless chair on runners, made to be pulled by one or two dogs. Any more dogs and you risk being out of control! Basket sleds, in which the basket is set high above the runners, are next in weight. They are fast, easy to manage and ideal for recreational mushing with a few dogs. Finally, toboggan sleds, in which the load is carried only inches above the runners, are the choice for soft snow and added stability, as well as for camping and long-distance trips. Both basket and toboggan sleds have simple but effective brakes.

Next you need harnesses for every dog in the team. A good fit is critical for your dogs' comfort and pulling ability. The harness of choice for speed or recreational mushing is the custom-fitted X-back harness with padding around the front. For heavier loads, a weight pulling (or freighting) harness is preferred, which is the same kind of harness used in competitive weight pulling. These harnesses have a wooden rod (called a spacer) at the rear that helps distribute the weight for ultimate pulling ability.

Ganglines (towlines, tuglines and necklines) attach the sled to the dogs' harnesses. The towline runs between all the pairs of dogs back to the sled, and tuglines run from each dog's harness to the towline. The neckline runs from the dog's collar to the towline, but is only there to keep all the dogs facing in the same direction—not for pulling. *Never* use cheap lines, and when possible, carry spares.

You'll also need a snow hook, which you'll be grateful for as your dogs are flying down the trail and your sled is careening behind them and your cries of "whoa!" are going unheeded. A snowhook is a big, heavy metal hook attached to the rear of the gangline that you can jab into the snow to try to slow your progress. It's more often used, however, as an anchor when you need to be off the sled while the dogs are stopped and you wish them to remain where they are rather than taking off without you.

You should also have lots of snug-fitting cordura or polar fleece dog booties to protect each dog's paws from injury and wear, particularly on icy snow or long trips. They are also essential for running on chemically treated or snowless ground.

Finally, what will you do if one of your dogs gets injured on the trail? A sled bag enables you to carry a dog on the sled without the dog jumping out. It's essential when you're anywhere away from civilization.

## Sledding Resources

### Books

Collins, M. and J., *Dog Driver. A Guide for the Serious Musher*, Alpine Publications, 1991.

Flanders, N.K., *The Joy of Running Sled Dogs*, Alpine Publications, 1989.

Levorsen, B. (ed), *Mush! A Beginner's Manual of Sled Dog Training*, Sierra Nevada Dog Drivers, Arner Publications, 1976.

Welch, J. *The Speed Mushing Manual: How to Train Racing Sled Dogs*, Sirius Publishing, 1989.

### Websites

Expedition Outfitters: www.expeditionoutfittersonline.com

Sled Dog Central: www.sleddogcentral.com

Dog Sled: www.dogsled.com

### Magazines

Mushing Dog Magazine: (907) 479-0454; www.mushing.com

### Sledding Vacations

www.sleddogcentral.com/rides&tours.htm

www.mushing.com/tours.htm

Once you have your equipment, it's time to teach your dog to pull. Get him used to the harness, and then to pulling a lightweight cart or sled. An experienced musher is invaluable as a guide, especially if your dog can learn by running as part of an experienced team—as long as that team is small, slow and easygoing. If no other help is available, start by training your sled dog using the same methods as you would for a skijor dog, but use skis only if you're an experienced skier and only with one or at most two dogs at a time. If no snow is available, use an all-terrain vehicle or a cart made just for this purpose, available from sledding outfitters. But be careful: Lightweight carts can go faster than you'd like to go on hard ground!

A sport would have to be pretty wonderful to attract so many people when it takes so much money and commitment. Dog sledding *is* pretty wonderful. It's you and your dogs alone on a snowy trail, silent but for the panting of the dogs and the cadence of their footfalls. Sledding combines excitement with beauty and the chance to be a team with your dogs in a way few people ever experience.

## PUT THE DOG BEFORE THE CART
### CARTING
**Abilities:** Knowledge of pulling commands

Haven't you dreamed of riding like royalty as your dog hauls you around in your carriage? Keep dreaming, because dog carting doesn't really work like that. You have to do your part for it to look easy. You also need to be realistic about your own weight. Don't expect your Pekingese to tow you around in a rickshaw. But small dogs can tow children's toys and wagons, medium dogs can tow children and large dogs can tow adults.

Start with a good harness; some vendors even sell harnesses that fit small dogs. Several styles are available. A *parade* harness has one strap that encircles the dog's chest and back, and another that wraps around the dog's forechest. Some dogs find the strap around the forechest restrictive. A *Siwash* harness has several straps across the dog's back and a strap that goes along the breastbone between the front legs and attaches to a belly band. It's more like a sled dog harness and allows the dog freer movement. A *draft* harness looks more like a draft horse's harness, with a large padded collar the dog can essentially lean into. It is connected to the dog by way of a belly strap.

Your choice of cart will depend on what you want to do. If you want your dog to help with yard work, choose a wagon with four wheels for stability. If you want your dog to give rides to the kids, a two-wheeled cart with a seat is a better choice. They're easier to maneuver than wagons, but they also tip more easily, so they should be reserved for dogs who already

### Carting Resources

Carting With Your Dog:
www.cartingwithyourdog.com

Carts: www.dogworks.com

Dog Carts: www.dogcarts.com

know how to pull. When loading a two-wheeled cart, remember that the weight must be balanced carefully over the axle so it doesn't bear down on the dog or tip to the rear. You can buy an expensive professionally made rig, or you can build one yourself. Unless you're very handy, buying one will save you a lot of frustration.

Begin training by putting the harness on your dog and getting her used to it without anything attached. Once she's walking comfortably in harness, hitch up the wagon or cart and walk alongside to help her out. Give her an incentive to walk forward, using lots of praise and treats. Use the pulling commands listed on page 109. Gradually add weight, and be sure to go somewhere. Make every hitch-up an adventure so she comes to look forward to it. Nobody likes walking in a circle.

Once she gets good at pulling, it's time to show off. Your dog can be the hit of any parade by pulling a cart with a child or even another dog in it.

## THAT DOG CAN HUNT

### HUNTING

**Abilities:** Varies

Dogs are hunters at heart. Many of their favorite games stem from their yen to chase and catch. Some of the earliest bonds between humans and dogs no doubt were forged in the mutual pursuit of some elusive quarry. That bond of hunting dog to hunting person still exists today, and many people find the best times they spend with their dogs are the times they spend together in the field.

Dogs who were bred for particular purposes are seldom happier than when they get to perform those functions, and many dog breeds owe their existence to hunting. Pointers love to search the brush for birds, Beagles are enraptured by the scent of a cottontail and Greyhounds find ecstasy in the pursuit of a hare.

But not all hunting dog owners are hunters at heart. That's OK. They can still spend time in the

**Squirrel Dog Resources**

Curs and Feists: www.ukcdogs.com/curfeist.html

Squirrel Dogs: www.sqdog.com

## Gun Dog Resources

Bird Dog & Retriever News: www.bird-dog-news.com

Bird Dogs Forever: www.birddogsforever.com

Bird Dog Training Links: www.mts.net/~oakgrove/point/trainlnk.html

Field Dog www.fielddog.com

Gun Dogs Online: www.gundogsonline.com

Hunting Dogs: www.huntingdogs.com

Hunting Links: www.hunttheworld.net

North American Hunting Retriever Organization: www.nahra.org

North American Versatile Hunting Dog Association: www.navhda.org

Pointing Dogs: www.pointingdogs.com

Retriever Guide: www.retrieverguide.com

Spaniel Journal: www.spanieljournal.com

Sporting Dogs: www.sportingdogs.com

Total Retriever: www.totalretriever.com

Upland Bird Dogs: www.uplandbirddog.com

Versatile Sporting Dogs: www.versatiledogs.com

Working Retriever Central: www.working-retriever.com

field with their canine companions but without harming other animals. Nonhunting Pointer people can do everything a hunter would do, except shoot the birds their dogs discover. Nonhunting Beagle people can still let their dog follow a trail without shooting the rabbit. Even nonhunting Greyhound people can make sure the hare gets a sufficient head start so it is certain to escape.

Some people hunt with dogs because they see the dogs as tools. Others hunt with dogs because they see the experience as a special time together. They use hunting as an excuse to get out in the field and slog around with their dogs under the pretense

## Sighthound Hunting Resources

Coursing Description: http://personal.palouse.net/valeska/ofc-article.htm

Coursing Overview:
www.borzoiclubofamerica.org/openfield.shtml

Lurchers and Staghounds: www.users.daelnet.co.uk/lurchers/

National Coursing Club (U.K.):
www.nationalcoursingclub.freeserve.co.uk/

National Open Field Coursing Association: www.nofca.cc/

that they have some sort of goal. These are the people (and dogs) this section is for.

The type of hunting you'll pretend to do depends on the type of hunting dog you pretend to have. Hunting dogs are divided into groups of hunting types, and even within those groups different breeds or strains have different hunting styles. Here's a rundown:

- **Gundogs** are breeds that help people hunt birds, either by pointing, flushing, retrieving or some combination of these tasks. Pointing dogs range back and forth, scenting for birds and freezing when they locate them. Flushing dogs locate and then flush birds skyward so the hunter can shoot the birds in flight. Retrieving dogs bring back downed birds from land or water.

- **Hounds** were developed to pursue furred quarry. Hounds are divided into sighthounds and scenthounds.

  **Sighthounds** pursue swift quarry by sight, overtaking it by means of their great speed. They are made up of the Greyhound-type dogs. Hunting with sighthounds in the United States usually means open field coursing, in which dogs chase jackrabbits in the open areas of the West.

## Scenthound Hunting Resources

AKC Basset Field Trials: www.akc.org/dic/events/perform/ftbasset.cfm

AKC Coonhound Events: www.akc.org/dic/events/perform/coonhounds/index.cfm

American Beagler Magazine: www.americanbeagler.net/aba.html

American Hunting Basset Association: www.bassetnet.com

American Rabbit Hound Association: www.arha.com

Basset Field Trials: www.basset.net/field.html

Basset Hound Hunting: www.basset.net/peg1.html

Beagle Hunting: www.iwbeagles.co.uk/

Beagles Unlimited: www.beaglesunlimited.com

Beagling: www.beaglesinperil.org.uk/beagling.htm

Coondogs: www.coondogs.net

Coonhound Central: www.coonhounds.com

Coonhound Nite Hunts: www.bordway.org/index.htm

Coonhound Water Races: www.ukcdogs.com/rules/ch-water.html

Foxhound Club of North America: www.fcna.com

Hunting Beagles: www.hunting.beagles.com

Masters of Foxhounds: www.mfha.com

Rabbit Hunting Online: www.rabbithuntingonline.com

Small Pack Option: www.espomagazine.com

UKC Coonhounds: www.ukcdogs.com/coonhound.shtml

**Scenthounds** follow quarry by their scent trail, usually pursuing it until it goes to ground or is treed. They are made up of Coonhound-, Foxhound-, Beagle- and Basset Hound–type dogs. Hunting with them varies according to the breed of dog. Coonhounds hunt at

### Working Terrier Resources

American Working Terrier Association: www.dirt-dog.com/awta/index.shtml

Dirt Dog: www.dirt-dog.com

Earth Dog and Running Dog: www.earthdogrunningdog.com

Hunting Terriers: www.terrierman.com

Jack Russell Trials: www.terrier.com/trial/trailing.php3

Working Terrier: www.workingterrier.com

night, baying as they follow the trail of a raccoon until the raccoon takes refuge up a tree. Foxhounds are most known for hunting in large packs followed by hunters on horseback, but Foxhounds may also hunt amid less elaborate trappings. Beagles and Bassets hunt rabbits while the people follow along on foot.

- **Terriers** were developed to pursue their quarry into burrows, either trapping it in a den or going in after it to dispatch it. They tend to catch or corner animals that fight back, including foxes, rats and badgers. Many specialize in working in close quarters, often deep underground.

Some dogs fall between these precise categories, and some dogs specialize in types of big-game hunting that are not compatible with spending a relaxing and safe day in the field with your dog.

Remember, you can shoot with a camera as easily as (and more safely than) with a gun, and you can usually arrange for any quarry to escape unscathed. Your dog may shake his head at your ineptitude, but he'll forgive you because for him, too, the thrill is in the chase and the excuse to share an outdoor adventure with you.

## Search and Rescue Resources

American Rescue Dog Association: www.ardainc.org

Cadaver Dog Training: www.cadaverdog.com

Canine Search and Recovery: www.csar.org

Jonni Joyce Seminars and Articles: www.jonnijoyce.com

National Disaster Search Dog Foundation: www.ndsdf.org

Rescue Net Training Classes: www.rescuenet.org/ricanine.htm

SAR Dogs Resources: www.sar-dogs.com

SAR Equipment: www.icsinternet.com/sarstore/

SAR FAQs: www.wtp.net/ASDK9SAR/faq.html

SAR Training Articles: www.wtp.net/ASDK9SAR/ newpage/page2.html

Search and Rescue Dog News: www.sardog.org

U.K. National Search and Rescue Dog Association: www. nsarda.org.uk

## RESCUE ME!

### SEARCH AND RESCUE

**Abilities:** Basic obedience, scent work

How about a little hero worship? Your dog can be somebody's hero by finding a child lost in the wilderness, a skier buried in an avalanche, a disaster victim covered by rubble or a senior with Alzheimer's lost in the neighborhood. You can add purpose to your jaunts through the wild by training your dog to be a search and rescue (SAR) dog. Even a city dog can become an urban searcher.

An SAR dog must respond reliably to commands, negotiate precarious footing, follow a trail and locate articles, and use air scenting to pinpoint the location of a hidden person. She must be hardy, strong, nimble, intelligent, friendly, dependable and brave. But an SAR dog is only half the team. An SAR handler must be trained in search techniques, compass and map reading, wilderness survival, first aid and a variety of other skills—not to mention being pretty hardy and rugged themselves. Both dog and person must be able to work through physical and emotional hardship.

So you think you and your dog have what it takes? Not so fast! You will have to train and prepare, and this is not something you can do alone. The best way to get started is to join a group where more experienced people can guide you. National and local SAR dog groups will usually meet for several hours a couple of times a month. You will have to train on your own in between. And remember, disasters don't just happen in nice weather or on weekends. You'll need to be ready to go whenever you're called—somebody's life may depend on it. It's a huge commitment of time, effort and even money. But it's an even huger payoff in the excitement of the search, the elation of the find and the deepening of the bond you share with your canine partner.

# Chapter 7

# The Best Organized Sports

Sharing a run in the wilds, a spot on the sofa or a treat from the drive-through—no dog lover will deny that these simple pleasures are the most important ones. But it would be a rare person who would not confess that at times, while watching their dog standing at attention gazing into the distance or doing something particularly clever, they've thought their dog is prettier and smarter than the average dog. Some people even set out to prove it, and that's where dog sports come into play.

But what do you really prove by competing? Perhaps you have some ribbons, an occasional trophy—maybe even a title to add to your dog's name. But that's not what you do it for. You do it for the car trips that start at unholy hours, the excursions to exotic fairgrounds, the chance to get lost on remote country roads and to discover that some judges are obviously not right in the head. Well, maybe that's not what you do it for, either.

So why do people really get involved in dog sports? Canine competitions give you a chance to share something special, to

## Competing with Mixed Breeds

Some competitions only allow dogs of certain breeds to compete, and many require the dogs to be registered with the organization sponsoring the event. That's especially true with conformation shows, but the rule is more flexible when it comes to performance and fun events. For example, although the American Kennel Club (AKC) allows only AKC-recognized breeds, you can get an Indefinite Listing Privilege (ILP) number for your unregistered purebred and compete in any AKC activity except conformation. And any dog, pure or mixed, can earn an AKC Canine Good Citizen title.

The United Kennel Club (UKC) allows mixed breeds to enter obedience and other performance events. The National Canine Association has special classes for mixed breeds. Even the Australian Shepherd Dog Club of America offers obedience titles to non-Aussies, including mixed breeds. So when in doubt, ask! Start with these:

American Mixed Breed Obedience Registry
179 Niblick Rd. #113
Paso Robles, CA 93446
(805) 226-9275
www.amborusa.org

Mixed Breed Dog Club of America
13884 State Route 104
Lucasville, OH 45648-8586
(740) 259-3941
www.mbdca.org

National Canine Association
6734 Huntsman Blvd.
Springfield, VA 22152
(703) 451-1948
www.nationalcanine.com

Australian Shepherd Club of America
6091 Hwy 21
Bryan, TX 77803-9652
(409) 778-1082
www.asca.org

Canine Performance Events: www.k9cpe.com

Great American Mutt Show
(212) 327-3164
www.greatamericanmuttshow.com

meet other people who embrace your interests, to forge special memories of your experiences with your dog and to memorialize your dog in some special ways.

Fortunately, just about every dog can excel in some sport. Sometimes it takes awhile to find just the right one for your dog, so here's a dog sports sampler to get you started.

## CITIZEN K-9
### CANINE GOOD CITIZEN TESTS

You and your dog are out for a stroll. A friendly stranger approaches and shakes your hand. He pets your dog as she sits and then examines her ears, feet and coat, even brushing her gently. This guy's getting kind of personal, but your dog is sitting politely and acting neither shy nor resentful. You're relieved that she's clean and parasite-free, and at a pretty decent weight. As you leave she walks politely on a loose leash, turning and stopping with you. Even when you walk through a group of several other people she doesn't pull, jump on them or act overly exuberant, shy or resentful. When she passes another dog and person, she shows only casual interest in the other dog. And she reacts calmly to a dropped chair and a passing jogger without panicking, barking or acting aggressively. Such a good girl!

You need to leave her for a moment, so you help her sit and tell her to stay as you walk 20 feet away and back. Then you walk 10 feet away and call her to you. Finally, you go out of her sight for three minutes, asking a stranger to hold her. She waits nicely, without constantly barking, whining or pacing. She makes you proud!

And you should be proud of her, because she's the type of dog who's a pleasure to take out in public, the type of dog who gives dogs a good name. She's a Canine Good Citizen (CGC) and she just passed the test to prove it.

Any dog, whether of mixed or pure heritage, is eligible for the CGC. Puppies can earn the title as soon as they are old enough to meet the vaccination requirement. Unlike formal obedience, you can talk to your dog throughout the test and precision isn't necessary. Bring your dog's buckle or slip collar, brush or comb, leash and proof of rabies vaccination. All the tests are done on a leash; a long line is provided for the stay and recall exercises.

To find a test in your area, go to www.akc.org or call the AKC at (919) 816-3532. If no test is scheduled, consider getting a group of friends together and asking a local tester to arrange one. Announce the test and invite other dogs to enter. Make an event of it!

## STEADY AS SHE GOES
### TEMPERAMENT TESTS

You're taking a casual walk in the park with your dog when a stranger approaches you to chat and shake hands. Later another stranger approaches and pets your dog. Your dog reacts calmly to both. As you continue to walk somebody rattles a metal bucket filled with rocks and then sets it in the path. Your dog investigates the bucket only when you allow him to. Then three gunshots ring out from behind you. Your dog jumps but recovers his composure.

As your walk continues, you approach a person sitting in a chair who points an umbrella at your dog and opens it. Your dog is again startled, but investigates only when told he can do so. You walk on and find you must cross over 15 feet of clear plastic and then 12 feet of an unfolded wire exercise pen. Your dog gives them a curious sniff but continues. Now a weird-looking person crosses the path in front of you. Your dog looks. Then the stranger advances on you threateningly. Your dog begins to act cautious or protective. Good boy! It's been a pretty exciting walk, but your dog has shown that he has the stuff to pass a Temperament Test.

The American Temperament Test Society (P.O. Box 4093, St. Louis, MO 63136, 314-869-6103; www.atts.org) sponsors temperament tests to evaluate a dog's stability and breed-appropriate behavior in some novel (I hope!) situations. Dogs who pass can add the Temperament Test (TT) title to the their names.

## SHOW OFF!
### CONFORMATION SHOWS

You stand at ringside and eye the competition. You just know your dog is better put together. And she's so clean her own mother wouldn't recognize her. Then you spot danger: a kid coming your way balancing a soda—barely. You're saved when the steward calls out "Open Bitches, 10, 12, 14, 16." That's you! You walk into the ring and you're in your first dog show.

You pose her just like you've practiced, with her front legs straight and parallel, her rear legs parallel also and her hocks perpendicular to the ground. You encourage her to hold her head up and look attentive at the piece of liver you're holding. Now the judge is telling you to take them all around—you remind yourself to keep her at a lively trot as you circle the ring. So far so good.

Now for the hard part: the individual exam. You pose her again as the judge takes a good look and then approaches her to examine her teeth and feel her underlying structure. She starts to wiggle and her tail wags out of control by the time the judge is finished. He smiles and asks you to take her down and back. Not too fast, you tell yourself, and you trot in such a straight line you could be on a balance beam—directly away and back to the judge, letting her stop and pose herself when you return. Another circle around the ring, another chance to pose while he studies the whole class, and suddenly you're being motioned to the first-place marker and handed a blue ribbon. Yippee!

But don't leave the ring yet. Now you have to compete against the other class winners, from Puppy, 12-to-18-Month, Novice, American-Bred, and Bred by Exhibitor for the coveted Winners award. It all goes quickly, and before you were even ready he's pointing at you again: Winners Bitch!

Before you can celebrate, you're reminded you need to stay in and compete for Best of Breed against the Winners Dog and all the Champions. You don't win that, but you're so busy hugging your dog and feeding her treats that you forget to wonder how many points she's won—until some people congratulate you and tell you she's won a three-point major! (It takes 15 points, including two majors—wins over entries large enough that they earn from three to five points—to become an AKC Champion.) You float in a daze around with your girl and visit the vendors' booths, where you buy her some treats and toys as her reward. Then you stay for the Group to root on your breed winner. The winner of each of the seven groups will go on to compete for Best in Show, but the Best-in-Show winner that day couldn't possibly be any more excited than you are.

Sound like fun? It would be if every dog won her first show like that. Of course, this almost never happens. But dog shows are fun anyway.

You can show your dog in conformation at shows sponsored by several dog organizations. Those held by the American Kennel Club are the most popular. To show in an AKC conformation show your dog must be at least six months old, registered with the AKC, neither spayed nor neutered and (if male) have two normally descended testicles. You must also make sure your dog doesn't have a disqualifying fault for her breed. (You find out about faults by reading the standard for your breed. A standard is a written description of the ideal dog of each breed, and at a conformation show the judge considers how well each dog conforms to the standard.) Other organizations have different requirements; some for example, allow spayed and neutered dogs to compete.

It will take many outings before both you and your dog will be able to give a polished performance. You can practice at informal matches meanwhile, and if you're lucky, join a handling class. Go to the AKC, UKC or other kennel club website for regulations and upcoming show listings.

Almost everyone who enters a dog show loses, because only one dog remains undefeated at the end of the show: the Best-in-Show winner. It can hurt to have your beloved friend walk out of the ring without a ribbon. Just be sure your dog doesn't pick up on your disappointment, and always treat her like a Best-in-Show winner whether she gets a blue ribbon or no ribbon at all. As long as you do that, you will always leave the show a winner.

## MIND GAMES
### OBEDIENCE TRIALS

"Are you ready?" the judge asks. Every part of you wants to scream "No!" "Yes," you reply. The judge says "Forward" and you tell your dog to heel. He does. The judge says "Halt" and you stop and your dog sits at your side. And so it continues. Fast and slow paces, left, right and about turns, even a figure 8 around two people. Then come the exercises he has to do off-lead. You step several feet away and he stands like a statue while the judge touches him. Good boy! He heels, drifts a little off course while he watches a dog in another ring, but recovers quickly and is back at your side. You see the judge make a few marks on his notepad—deductions from the perfect 200 score—but so far he is passing.

## Dog Showing Resources

### Books

Coile, D.C., *Show Me! A Dog Showing Primer*, Barron's, 1997.

Hall, Lynn, *Dog Showing for Beginners*, Howell Book House, 1994.

### Magazines

Dogs in Review: www.dogsinreview.com

Canine Chronicle: www.caninechronicle.com

### Websites

AKC Dog Competition Site: www.akc.org/dic/index.cfm

American Rare Breed Association: www.arba.org

Canadian Kennel Club: www.ckc.ca

Federation Cynologique Internationale: www.fci.be

International All Breed Canine Association: www.international dogshow.com

National Breed Clubs: www.netpets.com/dogs/dogclub.html

National Canine Association: www.nationalcanine.com

Show Dog Online Magazine: www.showdog-magazine.com

Show Dog Super Site: www.showdogsupersite.com

States Kennel Club: www.rarebreed.com/skc_shows.html

Superintendents: www.akc.org/dic/events/super.cfm

The Virtual Dog Show: www.dogshow.com

United Kennel Club: www.ukcdogs.com

Westminster Kennel Club: www.westminsterkennelclub.org

World Wide Kennel Club: www.worldwidekennel.qpg.com

You place him on a sit and walk to the other side of the ring, wait for the judge to tell you to call him—and he comes right to you and sits in front. Yes! He finishes the exercise by circling to the heel position, you wait for the judge to say "Exercise over" (as you do after every exercise) before you praise your dog, and you leave the ring to await the group exercises.

You let him rest while a few other dogs do their individual routines. One manages to fail by acting deaf when asked to come, and another is just so sloppy her owner is obviously concerned she may fall below the 170-point total needed to qualify, but finally they call about 10 dogs into the ring. The dogs sit next to one another as their owners leave them and stand on the other side of the ring while the dogs remain sitting for a minute. Then they do it again while the dogs lie down for three minutes. These aren't normal minutes. They're obedience ring minutes—the longest minutes on this planet. People age at three times the normal rate during obedience minutes. But somehow your dog stays for the required eternities, and you leave the ring ecstatic that he's earned a green ribbon and one of three qualifying scores, or legs, toward his AKC Companion Dog (CD) title.

Afterward you drift over to the Open ring, where you just may enter once you've conquered the Novice ring. Here the dogs are doing all the exercises off-lead and they're not only heeling but retrieving a dumbbell, even over a jump. They're dropping into a down in the middle of coming when called, and their group exercises are done with handlers out of the room and last three minutes for the sit and five minutes for the down. Obedience minutes. OK, maybe you can do that.

If they qualify in Open three times they earn the AKC Companion Dog Excellent (CDX) title, and get to move on to Utility. Those dogs are scary-smart! They're working only from hand signals, jumping and retrieving in different directions, and even choosing articles touched by their handlers from among unscented articles. If they pass three times they're awarded the Utility Dog (UD) title. Some of them are already Utility Dogs who are continuing to compete for high scores. If they score high enough they'll place first or second in their class and earn points toward the 100 points needed for an Obedience Championship, or OTCH—a certificate of true genius in the dog world. If they qualify in both Open and Utility on the same day at 10 different shows after earning a UD, they can earn a Utility Dog Excellent (UDX) title. And if they earn the highest score of any dog in the trial, no matter what regular class they're in, they're awarded the

High in Trial (HIT). But today you're just as happy with your first leg in Novice.

But what if you've never been good at taking orders? That obedience judge telling you what to do can make you a nervous wreck. Rally Obedience is your answer. Sure, the judge tells you when to start, but after that you follow directions from sign to sign. Directions like "Sit," "Take a step to the side," "Spiral" and "Jump." And unlike traditional obedience, you can praise and talk to your dog the whole time! Precision is not a major component in scoring. More important is that the dog demonstrates willingness and enjoyment while performing basic obedience tasks that every good companion should know.

If you enter any obedience competition with your dog, remember that failing a trial, in the scope of life, is an insignificant event. Never let a ribbon or a few points become more important than a trusting relationship with your companion. Besides, the times you and your dog failed spectacularly will make the best stories—and the best memories—in years to come.

## Leaps of Faith
### Agility Trials

You've walked the course so you know what to expect. Still, you do one last mental run-through to calm your nerves. Your dog isn't nervous at all; she's raring to go! You get the go-ahead and you race onto the course heading for the first jump: a double-bar jump just like the ones in the horse-jumping competitions. OK, a little lower. But it looms monstrously high now. Your dog soars over with air to spare. Now run with her to the broad jump . . . she's over!

Slow down now to climb the A-frame; you want her to touch the required contact points near the bottom going up and down. She does it! Another burst of speed to fly over the solid panel jump. Now through the tire jump. On to the pause table; you can see she's irritated that she has to stop and stay while the required five seconds tick off. But she does, and she leaps off determined to make up the time by hurtling through the curved 20-foot-long, two-foot-wide tunnel; you can almost hear her ricocheting off the sides in her eagerness.

# Obedience Resources

## *Books*

Burch, M. and Bailey, J., *How Dogs Learn,* John Wiley & Sons, 1999.

Reid, P., *Excel-Erated Learning: Explaining in Plain English How Dogs Learn and How Best to Teach Them,* James and Kenneth, 1996.

Handler, Barbara S., *Successful Obedience Handling: The New Best Foot Forward,* Alpine Publications, 1991.

Strickland, Winifred, *Expert Obedience Training for Dogs, 4th edition,* Howell Book House, 2003.

Tillman, P., *Clicking With Your Dog: Step-By-Step in Pictures,* Sunshine Books, 2001.

## *Websites*

Dog Obedience: www.k9web.com/dog-faqs/activities/obedience.html

The Dog Obedience and Training Page: www.dogpatch.org/obed

Dr. P's Dog Training: www.uwsp.edu/psych/dog/obed.htm

Clicker Projects: www.clickandtreat.com/ffbase.htm

See Kennel Club listings under Dog Showing Resources (page 131)

## *Magazines*

*Front and Finish*
P.O.Box 333, Galesburg, IL 61402-0333
(309) 344-1333
www.frontandfinish.com

*Off Lead*
6 State Rd. #113
Mechanicsburg PA 17050
(717) 691-3388
www.off-lead.com

Slow down now . . . another control obstacle. Walk slowly up the teeter-totter, wait for it to teeter so the other side comes down, and trot carefully down the other side, touching the contact point at the end. And another control obstacle: the dog walk. Climb a one-foot-wide panel up to about a person's height, walk across a solid bridge 10 feet or so long, and go down the other side. Now head to the closed tunnel . . . zoom! She runs blind through the fabric, confident that she will come out on the other side. Now race to the finish . . . oops, two more jumps one right after the other . . . she's over, and past the finish line! Barking with excitement, she adds a leap into your arms for good measure.

Not only did she ace every obstacle, but she did it well within the time limit and the audience is cheering her performance. Is it any wonder agility is the fastest growing dog sport in the world?

Your dog has earned one of three qualifying scores in Novice that she will need to get her Novice Agility (NA) title. But she still wants to play some more, and fortunately you've entered her in another class called Jumpers With Weaves (JWW). And that's her favorite because it doesn't have those pesky control obstacles where she has to touch contact points or pause. It's a class for canine adrenaline junkies who just like to tackle the fast parts of the course. And for added excitement, the dogs get to weave in and out of series of slalom poles as fast as they can. If she passes this class, too, she'll have a leg toward her Novice Agility Jumpers (NAJ) title. Then it's on to Open!

The Open class has more obstacles, including weave poles and often a triple-bar jump. Once she qualifies three times there she's awarded the Open Agility (OA), or for JWW, the Open Agility Jumper (OAJ) title. Then she can enter the Excellent class, which has even more obstacles. One day maybe she'll earn the Agility Excellent (AX) and Excellent Agility Jumper (AXJ), and even the Master Agility Excellent (MX) and Master Agility Jumper (MXJ). These courses get tougher not only because more obstacles are used, but because the course becomes more complex and challenging in its layout. For example, the obstacles may need to be approached from sharp angles (up to 90 degrees in Novice, 135 degrees in Open and 180 degrees in Excellent). Courses may also include call-offs, in which the dog must skip an obstacle in his

# Agility Resources

## Organizations

See contacts for the AKC and UKC under Dog Showing Resources (page 131)

United States Dog Agility Association
P.O. Box 850995
Richardson, TX 75085-0955
(972) 231-9700
www.usdaa.com

Agility Association of Canada
RR#2
Lucan, Ontario, N0N 2J0
(519) 657-7636
www.aac.ca

North American Dog Agility Council
HCR 2, Box 277
St. Maries, ID 83861
(208) 689-3803
www.nadac.com

Australian Shepherd Club of America
6091 East State Highway 21
Bryan, TX 77803-9652
(409) 778-1082
www.asca.org

## Books

Bonham, M. *Introduction to Dog Agility,* Barrons Educational Series, 2000.

path; options and traps, in which the dog must jump only one of two obstacles at a decision point; side-switches, in which the course makes an S curve, requiring the handler to switch from one side of the dog to the other; and lead-out advantages, in which handlers who can run ahead of their dogs while the dog remains steady at the start line or pause table are at an advantage. That's going to take some practice for both of you!

Simmons-Moake, J. *Dog Agility: The Fun Sport for All Dogs,* Howell Book House, 1992.

Simmons-Moake, J. *Excelling at Dog Agility I: Obstacle Training,* Flash Paws, 1999.

Simmons-Moake, J. *Excelling at Dog Agility II: Sequence Training,* Flash Paws, 2000.

## Magazines

*Clean Run*
35 North Chicopee St., Unit 4
Chicopee, MA 01020
(800) 311-6503
Outside the U.S.: (413) 532-1389
www.cleanrun.com

## Websites

The Dog Agility Page: www.dogpatch.org/agility

Dog Agility for Novices: www.agilitytrial.com

Clean Run Productions: www.cleanrun.com

Agility Training Tips: www.netscenes.com/pawsabilities/training.htm

Affordable Agility Equipment: www.affordableagility.com

Like any athlete, your dog must be in peak physical condition to compete in agility. You also need to have a health check beforehand, making sure your dog is not dysplastic, arthritic or visually impaired. High jumping and vigorous weaving can impose stresses on immature bones, so these activities should be left until adulthood.

The AKC, United States Dog Agility Association (USDAA) and United Kennel Club (UKC) are the major sponsors of agility trials in the United States, and many other countries have their own versions. The rules may differ slightly, but the concept, excitement and fun level are the same.

## LED BY THE NOSE

### TRACKING TRIALS

The air is gray with the morning mist—so gray your dog is just a shadow up ahead as he ranges in search of a scent. He exhales with a snort and strikes off decisively toward a grove across the field. You play out more line and let him guide you along a trail you can't see but he can smell, as confident in his decision as a sightless person is with a guide dog—because in the world of scenting, you might as well be blind.

The track was laid by a person 30 minutes to two hours ago and you know it's between 440 to 500 yards. But every yard followed blindly is a long one. Your dog has done it before, but always in practice. This morning is different. This morning is a real trial, and if he follows the track to its end just one time he will earn the Tracking Dog (TD) title.

You think ahead to the next challenge: The Tracking Dog Excellent (TDX) title is earned by following an older (three to five hours) and longer (800 to 1,000 yards) track with five to seven turns, with more challenging circumstances. One of these circumstances is the existence of cross-tracks laid by another tracklayer after the first track was lain. In addition, the actual track may cross various types of terrain and obstacles, including plowed land, woods, streams, bridges and lightly traveled roads.

Then there's the Variable Surface Tracking (VST) title, earned by following a three- to five-hour track, 600 to 800 yards long, over a variety of surfaces such as sand, asphalt, rock, grass and even through buildings—surfaces that may be crossed by animal, pedestrian or vehicular traffic.

You're snapped back to reality by a sudden surge of your dog as he races toward an object on the ground. He's found the glove that marks the end of the trail! He's a Tracking Dog!

### Tracking Resources

#### Books

Button, Lou, *Practical Scent Dog Training*, Alpine Publications, 1990.

Johnson, Glen R., *Tracking Dog: Theory & Methods*, Barkleigh Productions, 1999.

Sanders, William R., *Enthusiastic Tracking: The Step-by-Step Training Manual*, Rime Publications, 1998.

#### Websites

AKC Tracking Rules: www.akc.org/dic/events/obedtrack/trackreg.cfm

Dr. P's Tracking Links: www.uwsp.edu/psych/dog/Work2.htm

The Tracking Page: http://personal.cfw.com/~dtratnac/

Tracking Dog Pages: home.wanadoo.nl/stroomh/

Tracking: www.basset.net/track.html

## TO SERVE AND PROTECT
### SCHUTZHUND TRIALS

He knows his job, and when you send him to search he approaches each hiding place boldly. Finding nobody in the first one, he strides to a second and barks to alert you to the presence of a person hiding, dressed in heavy padding. You come to escort the man away, but as you're walking the man attacks you. Your dog hurls himself on the man, grabbing him by the padded arm and holding him in place, even when the man turns on the dog and hits him twice with a padded stick. Later the man tries to flee, but your dog runs him down and subdues him. Will this guy never learn? Lucky for him your dog releases him as soon as you give the command. Lucky for you your dog is passing the protection phase of his Schutzhund test.

*Schutzhund,* which is German for "protection dog," tests tracking, obedience and protection abilities all in the same day. Schutzhund trials are both popular and controversial. This controversy is in part due to a public misconception that Schutzhund dogs are simply attack dogs. Attack or protection training without obedience training is not Schutzhund! You're better off not training your dog at all than training him only for protection work without the obedience.

Before competing in a Schutzhund trial, a dog must pass the *Begleithunde* (or companion dog) test, which consists of a basic obedience evaluation and a demonstration that he's under control around joggers, bicyclists, cars, unfamiliar dogs and loud noises. The Schutzhund trial itself begins with a brief temperament evaluation to weed out aggressive or uncontrollable dogs. Dogs can progress from the easiest Schutzhund title (SchH1) through SchH2 to the most difficult level, SchH3.

The ScH1 title requires the dog to follow your own short, freshly laid track and to perform some obedience exercises. The obedience includes heeling on and off leash (at some point ignoring gunshots), sitting and downing from a walk at heel, staying, coming, retrieving over a flat surface and a jump, and going ahead of the handler for 25 paces and lying down on command. He must also pass a protection test, in which he must search two blinds (small structures behind which a person can hide), and when he finds the "helper" (a threatening or attacking person dressed in heavy padding) the dog must hold him in position by barking. When the helper attacks the handler, the dog must attack and hold the helper by biting him, even when the helper hits the dog twice with a padded stick. The dog must pursue and attack the fleeing helper. In all cases, the dog must release the helper immediately when the handler tells him to do so.

For the SchH2, the trail for tracking is slightly longer and older, and is laid by a stranger. Its obedience phase adds a retrieve over a five-foot wall and substitutes heavier articles to retrieve. For the SchH2 degree, the dog must search six blinds. Upon finding the helper, the dog must bark but return to the handler when commanded. When the helper tries to escape, the dog must stop him by biting hard and must release when the helper freezes. The dog should again bite the helper when the helper threatens the dog with a padded stick. The dog must watch the helper as the

## Protection Sport Resources

### Books

Barwig, Susan and Hilliard, Stewart, *Schutzhund: Theory and Training Methods*, Howell Book House, 1991.

Balabanov, Ivan and Duet, Karen, *Advanced Schutzhund*, Howell Book House, 1999.

### Websites

American Working Dog Federation: www.awdf.net

Dog Sports Magazine: www.dogsports.com

DVG America: www.dvgamerica.com

French Ring Sport: www.members.aol.com/malndobe/frring.htm

North American Ring Association: www.ringsport.org

United Schutzhund Dog Clubs of America: www.german shepherddog.com

United States Mondioring Association: www.usmondioring.org

Working Dogs Cyberzine Schutzhund Archives: www.workingdogs.com/articles_schutz.htm

handler searches him. The dog then walks next to the handler as they escort the helper ahead of them; when the helper turns and tries to attack the handler, the dog must stop the helper by biting.

For the SchH3, the track is even longer and older and requires the dog to locate three dropped articles. Its obedience exercises add a stop from both a walk and a run at heel while the handler continues on, substitutes an even heavier article for the flat retrieve, and a six-foot wall for the jump. For the SchH3 degree, the dog performs similar exercises as for the SchH2 but does the whole thing off-leash (some of the exercises in the lower levels are done on-leash).

Not tough enough for you? French Ring Sport or *mondioring* are the macho versions of Schutzhund—as if Schutzhund weren't sufficiently macho! Protection sports attract breeds that are used

### Water Test Resources

Dog Scouts Water Merit Badges: www.dogscouts.com/wet.shtml

Newfoundland Water Test: www.newfdogclub.org

Portuguese Water Dog Water Test: www.pwdca.org/water.html

WET DOG: www.wetdog.org

Breeds developed for water rescue, such as Newfoundlands (Newfoundland Club of America, 107 New St., Rehoboth, MA 02769, www.newfdogclub.org) and Portuguese Water Dogs (Portuguese Water Dog Club of America, www.pwdca.org) compete in water exercises that include retrieving. Some exercises are open to dogs of other breeds.

for police K-9 work, such as German Shepherd Dogs and Belgian Malinois, but several organizations allow any breed to compete. Still, a Schutzhund Shih Tzu seems unlikely.

## IN THE SWIM
### WATER TESTS

You're floundering around in the water, sinking beneath the surface then splashing your way back up. Suddenly you feel something brush against you—something big and furry and reassuring. You grab hold and he tows you to shore. You kneel beside him and give him a big hug—not because he saved your life, but because he's passed the last test to earn his Water Education and Training Excellent (WETX) title.

· Some breed clubs have their own water tests, but any dog can earn a Water Education and Training Dog Obedience Group (WET DOG) certificate. Allowances are made so that even small dogs can qualify—although don't depend on a toy dog to tow a boat to shore. To pass the basic level and earn the Water Education and Training Test (WETT) title, a dog must retrieve an object thrown into the water, retrieve an object dropped from a boat without seeing it dropped, tow a boat for 50 feet in chest-deep water, bring a line out to a person in the water and swim out with a person and then tow that person to shore. In addition, the dog has to pass the Novice level exercises for AKC obedience. For the advanced title of WETX your dog also needs to know how to distinguish a person in distress from one who doesn't need help, retrieve underwater and bring a boat paddle to a person in a boat.

## DOCK DOGS
### DOCK JUMPING COMPETITIONS

You shout "Let's dive!" and release your dog's collar. Both of you run toward the end of the 30-yard dock, where you fling her favorite retrieving dummy far out over the water. She's still gaining momentum as she catapults off the end of the dock into space, flying, soaring over the water for 20 feet or so before she lands with a tsunami splash. And comes up holding the dummy in her smiling mouth. You're smiling, too. That's the longest jump so far, and she's in good position to win the dock dog contest.

Dock dog contests, also known as Big Air contests, are won by the dog who jumps the farthest distance over the water after an object thrown by her handler. The dog lands (eventually) in the water and must bring the object to shore. But it's the jumping that's the fun part. For information, go to www.dockdogs. com or contact J4 Promotions, 5183 Silver Maple Lane, Medina, OH 44256, (330) 722-6363. Some training aids are available through www.sportmutts.com.

## FIELD OF DREAMS
### HUNTING TESTS AND TRIALS

You have a good hunting companion. In fact, your dog excels at what she was bred to do. Maybe she can tree a raccoon quicker than any of her hunting partners. Or freeze on point more reliably. Or follow a cottontail through impassable thickets. Or outrun a jackrabbit. Or excel at any of the many hunting jobs dogs have been doing for centuries. Chances are she can prove it at a field event, either a hunt test or a field trial. What's the difference? In general, a hunt test is a noncompetitive event in which dogs must perform up to a certain standard in order to pass, while a field trial is an event in which dogs compete against one another to earn placements and points. At AKC hunting tests dogs can earn the titles Junior Hunter, Senior Hunter and Master Hunter. At field trials they can earn the titles Field Champion or Amateur Field Champion. The UKC offers titles as well, as do several organizations that focus on only one breed or one aspect of the sport.

AKC pointing dog trials are open to Brittanys, English Setters, German Shorthaired Pointers, German Wirehaired Pointers, Pointers, Gordon Setters, Irish Setters, Vizslas, Weimaraners and Wirehaired Pointing Griffons. Dogs hunt in pairs and are judged on their ability to find and point birds and to retrieve downed birds.

AKC retriever hunting tests and field trials are open to Chesapeake Bay, Curly-Coated, Flat-Coated, Golden and Labrador Retrievers and Irish Water Spaniels. Dogs must retrieve downed birds from both land and water, with different testing levels requiring them to remember (or mark) increasingly difficult falls and multiple birds, and perform blind retrieves (find unmarked birds guided by their handler's directions, see page 130).

AKC spaniel hunting tests are open to Clumber, Cocker, English Cocker, English Springer, Field, Sussex and Welsh Springer Spaniels, with more highly competitive field trials also available to Cocker, English Cocker and English Springer Spaniels. The spaniels are tested on their ability to find, flush and retrieve game on both land and water.

Beagles have three kinds of AKC field trials: In Brace, the dogs run in sets of two or three dogs; in Small Pack Option (SPO), the dogs run in packs of seven; and in Large Pack all the dogs in the class run together. Beagles are judged on their ability and accuracy in finding and trailing rabbits. Basset Hounds and Dachshunds have similar events, but only run in Brace competitions.

Coonhounds (Black and Tan, Blue Tick, American, English, Redbone and Plott Hounds) have a wide choice of AKC and UKC competitions, including wild coon hunts, water races, treeing contests and drag races.

Sighthounds (Afghan Hounds, Azawakhs, Borzoi, Greyhounds, Ibizan Hounds, Irish Wolfhounds, Pharaoh Hounds, Salukis, Scottish Deerhounds, Sloughis and Whippets) can compete in open field coursing events in arid areas of the western United

## Hunting Test and Trial Resources

AKC Coonhounds: www.akc.org/dic/events/perform/coonhounds/index.cfm

AKC Performance Regulations: www.akc.org/insideAKC/regs.cfm

American Hunting Basset Association: www.bassetnet.com

American Rabbit Hound Association: www.arha.com

Basset Field Trials: www.basset.net/field.html

Beagle Small Pack Option: www.espomagazine.com

Coonhound Nite Hunts: www.bordway.org/index.htm

National Open Field Coursing Association: www.nofca.cc/

North American Hunting Retriever Organization: www.nahra.org

North American Versatile Hunting Dog Association: www.navhda.org

UKC Beagles: www.ukcdogs.com/beagle.html

UKC Coonhounds: www.ukcdogs.com/coonhound.shtml

Working Retriever Central: www.working-retriever.com

States in which two or three dogs attempt to catch jackrabbits that have been bolted from their natural hiding places.

Don't expect to qualify at your first test or trial (maybe not even your second—or seventh). You may, but chances are something will go wrong. Just look upon it as a chance to try again. Ask the advice of other participants and try to make some contacts with people who may help as training partners. Don't sweat it; while it's fun to bring home a ribbon, it's more gratifying to bring home the memories of a day in the field with a great dog.

## DRIVING AMBITIONS
### HERDING TESTS AND TRIALS

Somehow you never imagined you'd be walking into a pen of sheep with a dog at your side. She seems to be curious but calm as you lead her around on a leash. Her behavior is deemed acceptable and the leash is removed. She's at a Herding Instinct test to see if she has what it takes to be a natural herder. If she runs from the sheep or tries to attack them or just cowers at your feet, you can count that as a bad sign. But she doesn't. Whew!

The problem now is you don't know how to tell her what to do. Fortunately, the tester is used to guiding and evaluating new dogs, and he helps direct her actions. He makes notes on whether she has a tendency to move the stock either toward or away from you, whether she tends to run wide or close in relation to the stock, whether she moves from side to side to keep the stock together, whether she tends to have a strong eye (meaning she tends to move the stock with a stalking behavior), whether she is easily distracted, tends to bark or is overly aggressive, whether she responds to guidance and whether she is able to do a number of other things that good herding dogs do.

Your dog remains interested in the sheep. She's moving toward them slowly, staring them down without trying to chase them. In fact, she slows down when they start to move away too fast. She circles them at a distance, close enough that they keep an eye on her but far enough away that they don't try to bolt. Your 10 minutes in the sheep pen are up before you know it. The evaluator is filling out some paperwork—and smiling. So are you, and so is your dog. She's had a great time and she has a great future ahead of her.

True, she'll need some training before she can enter a herding trial or even a test. Herding tests are noncompetitive events in which dogs must exhibit a certain level of proficiency to pass. Herding trials are competitive events in which dogs are scored and placed in relation to one another.

You'll work toward the AKC Herding Tested (HT) title next, where she'll have to demonstrate her ability to move and control livestock by fetching or driving while working at the proper balance point required to move the stock. She'll have 10 minutes to move the stock three times between two pylons placed 10 feet from the fence at opposite sides of the arena. She'll conclude by responding to your commands to stop and to come. Once she passes twice, you can add the HT title after her name.

## Herding Resources

### Organizations

American Herding Breed Association
277 Central Ave.
Seekonk, MA 02771
www.ahba-herding.org

United States Border Collie Handlers' Association
2915 Anderson Lane
Crawford, TX 76638
www.usbcha.com

### Websites

German Shepherds Herding: www.geocities.com/Heartland/Ranch/5093/

Herding on the Web: www.glassportal.com/herding/index.html

Herding Organizations: www.glassportal.com/herding/programs.htm

Several organizations sponsor tests and trials. Although the general requirements are similar, each has enough differences that you should obtain the official rules from each organization. Caution: Herding is addictive! You may find yourself buying a farm so you can live with your own practice herds.

Different breeds have different herding styles. For example, Border Collies are known for their finesse, speed and intensity, and Australian Shepherds are known for their courage. Most herding trials favor such breeds. German Shepherds are known for their expertise in handling very large flocks in open areas, where they act almost like moving fences, constantly patrolling a boundary to prevent sheep from crossing. German Shepherds can demonstrate their ability to control large flocks in *Herdengebrauchshund* (Herding Utility Dog) trials. While AKC herding trials usually use flocks of 5 to 10 sheep, these trials use flocks of at least 200 sheep.

## Musical Freestyle Resources

### Organizations

Canine Freestyle Federation
21900 Foxden Lane
Leesburg, VA 20175
www.canine-freestyle.org

World Canine Freestyle Organization
P.O. Box 350122
Brooklyn, NY 11235-2525
(718) 332-8336
www.worldcaninefreestyle.org

### Websites

Freestyle: www.dog-play.com/musicall.html

Dogpatch Freestyle Page: www.dogpatch.org/obed/obpage6.cfm

## TWO RIGHT FEET
### DOGGY DANCING

The music starts. The crowd quiets. You bow to your partner. He bows back. The dance begins. You move gracefully across the floor, spinning, circling and side-stepping, both of you in sync with the other's movements. You've never had a better dance partner and the two of you have never danced so beautifully. The dance is over. The crowd applauds. You take a bow. He says "ruff!"

Several organizations sponsor canine musical freestyle competitions, with different rules but one overriding philosophy: teamwork can be beautiful. Some competitions emphasize heeling work to music, in which the dog should stay close to the person and avoid any fancy moves; it's sort of like cheek-to-cheek ballroom dancing. Then there's freestyle, in which the dog and handler may be widely separated as they perform more intricate and dazzling steps. It's more like modern dance.

Some organizations even offer competitions based on your performance you've sent in on videotape. There go your excuses about being shy or not being able to travel. Although once you've become a video star, you may be tempted to take to the stage.

## FLYING SAUCERS
### DISC DOG COMPETITIONS

A gentle breeze pushes billowy clouds across a tranquil sky. A disc floats high overhead and is suddenly snatched from midair by a leaping dog. The crowd cheers, another disc flies and the dog—your dog—leaps again to make an impossible catch. You already knew he was a flying star, but it makes you proud to show his stuff for the rest of the world to admire.

Canine Frisbee or flying disc contests are found all over the country, from local competitions to regional and national events. Several types of competition are offered.

In catch and retrieve (also known as mini-distance) competitions, the object is for a dog and handler team to make as many successful catches as possible in a minute, with extra points given for catches of longer throws. In freestyle (or freeflight) competitions, a dog and handler team perform a choreographed routine of tricks, often to music, for a minute. Competitors are judged on their teamwork, originality and athletic agility as they spin, twirl and leap to great heights in pursuit of the flying disc. In accuracy competitions, the team gets points when the dog makes a catch in one of four different-size circles placed at various distances from the thrower. Higher points are awarded to catches made in more distant circles. In long distance competitions, the dog who makes the catch at the greatest distance from the thrower wins.

You plan to win them all.

## CATCH IT!
### FLYBALL RELAYS

As your teammate's dog crosses the line for home, your dog crosses it heading for the hurdles. He leaps over the first low jump and then the next and the next and the next, taking only a single stride between them. He skids to a halt in front of a box

## Disc Dog Resources

### Organizations

Flying Disc Dog Open
P.O. Box 4615
Cave Creek, AZ 85327
(866) DISC-DOG
www.fddo.org

International Disc Dog Handlers' Association
1690 Julius Bridge Rd.
Ball Ground, GA 30107
(770) 735-6200
www.iddha.com

SkyHoundz
4060-D Peachtree Rd., Suite 326
Atlanta, GA 30319
(800) 786-9240
www.skyhoundz.com

### Websites

Disc Dog Page: www.discdog.com/FAQ.htm

Dogpatch Frisbee Page: www.dogpatch.org/dogs/frisbee.cfm

and slams onto its spring-loaded platform, positioning his mouth where he knows from experience the tennis ball launched by the box will fly. He ricochets off the box and with ball in mouth, rushes back to you, again taking the jumps with only a single stride between them. You're yelling, the opposing team is yelling and the crowd is going wild. Yes! He crosses the finish line first. He's the hero of the day but he doesn't care about that. He has a tennis ball!

Flyball is the most exciting canine team sport around, and while some dogs are better at it than others, any dog can play. It's a relay race in which two teams of four dogs each go head-to-head down a course of four low hurdles spaced 10 feet apart. Their goal is a box that shoots out a tennis ball when the dog steps on its spring-loaded platform. The dog catches the ball and

## Flyball Resources

North American Flyball Association (NAFA)
1400 W. Devon Ave., #512
Chicago, IL 60660
www.flyball.org
Flyball Homepage: www.flyballdogs.com

heads back to the starting line. When she crosses it the next dog on the team can start. The hurdle height is between 8 and 16 inches. Don't think your dog is too short to compete; most teams have one token short dog because the height of the hurdles is set at four inches below the shoulder height of the shortest dog on the team (down to eight inches).

Since this is a team sport, dogs earn points toward titles based on their team's times. Titles range from Flyball Dog (FD, 20 points) to Flyball Grand Champion (FDGCh, 30,000 points). If all four complete a course in less than 24 seconds, each dog earns 25 points; if it takes them less than 27 seconds they each earn five points; and if it takes them less than 32 seconds they each earn one point. Sound impossible? The record time is just over 16 seconds!

## THE ALLURE OF THE CHASE
### *LURE COURSING TRIALS*
You hold onto your hound as she strains and leaps in her efforts to be set free, until you release her at the hunt master's "Tallyho!" She and her two running mates burst from the slips to gain on the quarry, until it suddenly changes direction and leaves them slamming on the brakes and scrambling to turn and catch up. Straightaways, turns, acceleration, braking—the course continues until they finally turn back toward you. Now you can feel the ground rumbling under their pounding feet and see the excitement on their faces. As the object of the chase slows, the dogs snatch it triumphantly, every bit as proud as though they had filled the pot for a feast. Of course, the catch won't be very nutritious: It's simply a white plastic garbage bag.

## Lure Coursing Organizations

American Kennel Club Lure Coursing: www.akc.org/dic/events/
perform/lure1.cfm

American Sighthound Field Association
7045 SE 61st St.
Tecumseh, KS 66542
www.asfa.org

You wonder if your dog scored well. She was enthusiastic, fast and agile, she followed right after the lure and she didn't even tire near the end of the 700-yard course. She was clearly better than the competition. But can she do it again for her second required run? If so, she'll earn points toward her Field Championship and get to run against the winner of the Field Champion stake for Best of Breed. And the winner of that will go on to compete for Best in Field against the other breed winners.

You lead her from the field, her sides still heaving from exertion and her face aglow with excitement. The next course begins and she whips around toward the field: "Let's do it again!" She doesn't care how she scored. She just wants to run.

Sighthounds love to run and chase, and lure coursing gives them the perfect excuse. Lure coursing is a simulated hunting course in which a lure (actually a white plastic garbage bag) is dragged at high speed around a system of pulleys.

Of course, not all sighthounds consider a garbage bag suitable prey. You can test your dog's lure enthusiasm, and build it to a certain extent, with a pole lure (see page 172). Dogs who show an interest may be lure coursing prospects. They'll still need to practice on a real course, and they'll need to demonstrate they can run with another dog without chasing that dog or interfering with that dog's run. Some dogs don't understand that the way to win is by outrunning the other dogs, not by tripping them up!

Both the American Kennel Club (AKC) and the American Sighthound Field Association (ASFA) sponsor lure coursing field trials. Dogs run in groups of up to three and are scored on their speed, agility, endurance and ability to follow the lure, plus an additional category of either enthusiasm (for ASFA trials) or overall ability (for AKC trials). The AKC awards the Junior Courser (JC) title for a dog who demonstrates twice that he can finish a course running by himself, Senior Courser (SC) for a dog who receives four qualifying scores running with competition, Master Courser (MC) for dogs who earn an additional 25 qualifying scores, and Field Champion (FC) for dogs who accumulate 15 points including two firsts of at least three points. First-place dogs get points based on how many other dogs they defeated, for a maximum of five points per trial; second and third placements can also receive points.

The ASFA, which is the original sponsor of lure coursing in America, also awards a Field Champion (FCH) title for dogs who win 100 points, including two first (or one first and two second) placements over competition. They go on to award the extremely competitive Lure Courser of Merit (LCM) for winning an additional 300 points and four firsts from the FCH stake. Dogs can go on to win LCM2, LCM3 and so on for winning even more points and first placements.

## A RACING HEART
### AMATEUR RACING

"And they're off!" There he is, breaking late from the starting box. But he's gaining with every stride. You can't breathe. It's like you're running every stride with him. And he's gaining still: from fourth place to third to second but the track is only 200 yards and he's running out of track. He's neck and neck with the other dog as they cross the finish line. He wins! You rush to hug him and to stop him from trying to devour the lure through his muzzle!

Although amateur sighthound racing isn't yet available throughout the country, its objective nature—the winner is the first one over the finish line—safety and pure adrenaline rush promise to make it a growing sport. You can do your part by getting your sighthound race-ready now.

Besides needing a lure-savvy and clean running dog, you need your dog to be so enthusiastic that he ignores the muzzle he's required to wear. He also needs to practice breaking from a starting box a few times. Neither is difficult, as long as your dog

## Running Safety

Some owners are reluctant to try racing or coursing because they fear their dog could be injured. Fortunately, serious injuries are rare. You can do your part to reduce their likelihood by conditioning your dog.

Do not run your dog competitively if he does not get regular running conditioning during the week. If your dog has a previous injury, check with your veterinarian to make sure you don't risk reinjuring him. Always limber your dog up before running and walk him afterwards. If you expect to compete with your dog in an athletic event, be sure to treat him like the athlete he is.

Any kind of running activity is certainly more dangerous than snoozing on the couch, but everything worth doing in life comes with some risk. Is it worth it? Ask the people who drive hundreds of miles every weekend to stand in the rain and watch their dog run a course, even though they know their dog may have little chance of winning. They do it because they enjoy watching a beautiful animal do what he does best, and because they enjoy watching their beloved dogs do what they love most.

is crazy for the lure. Training to chase the lure starts with the pole lure (see page 172). In addition, dogs must learn to tolerate a racing muzzle. This is usually readily accepted if it's combined with the fun of chasing. Let the dog catch the lure and immediately pull the muzzle off so that he can grab the lure.

Only some races use starting boxes, but it's still a good idea to familiarize your dog with them. Start at home by walking your pup through a cardboard box. String the lure through it and practice letting your pup chase the lure through the box. Now loosely close the flap on the far end of the box and pull the lure through it. Raise the flap as the pup approaches. Gradually make your pup wait longer for the flap to be opened, and reward him with a frolic after the lure. Don't let your pup cheat by going around the box! Eventually you will need to practice with a real box and lure, but this at-home training will give your dog a good head start.

The largest number of racing events are held for Whippets, but the Large Gazehound Racing Association sponsors straight

## Amateur Racing Organizations

Jack Russell Terrier Club of America Trials
P.O. Box 4527
Lutherville, MD 21094-4527
(410) 561-3655
www.terrier.com

Large Gazehound Racing Association
1839 Mecklenburg Rd.
Ithaca, NY 14850
www.lgra.org

National Oval Track Racing Association: www.notra.org

North American Whippet Racing Association
1340 Shepherds Creek Dr.
Lucas, TX 75002
www.nawra.com

Whippet Racing Association
4300 Denison Ave.
Cleveland, OH 44109-2654
www.whippetracing.org

racing over a 200-yard course for other sighthounds. Racers earn points toward the Gazehound Racing Champion (GRC) title and then the Superior Gazehound Racing Champion (SGRC) title. The National Oval Track Racing Association sponsors oval racing over distances of at least 300 yards. It awards the titles of Oval Racing Champion (ORC) and Supreme Oval Racing Champion (SORC).

Racing isn't limited to sighthounds. Some of the most exciting races are at Jack Russell Terrier trials, where six terriers chase a lure down the track for about 200 feet and through a hole in some straw bales. The first dog through the hole is the winner. Races can be either flat races or steeplechases over six low hurdles. The whole race lasts only a few seconds—but they're six of the most exciting seconds in any dog sport!

## DOWN AND DIRTY
### EARTHDOG TRIALS

This seems crazy. Here you are holding your dog looking at a hole in the ground. You're 10 feet away from it and the judge is telling you to let your dog loose. Good thing the area is fenced! The dog bolts away in a random direction, and the judge beckons you to stand quietly beside the tunnel entrance. You do so, hoping that on one of his passes maybe your dog will accidentally fall in the hole. Luckily, he sees it in time. And stops. And sniffs. And pokes his head way down in there. And follows his head with the rest of his body, until his wagging tail disappears from view.

You imagine what it must be like under there. Dark and close, with an unfamiliar scent drawing him ever deeper into the tunnel. Until he comes face to face with an animal he's never encountered before except in the depths of his instinct-driven dreams: a rat! He's hesitant at first; he knows better than to bark at the cat at home. But he can't help himself, and he hurls threats at the rat, who nonchalantly chomps on some treats safely behind the bars that separate his cage from your canine predator. When he has given the rat a piece of his mind for 30 seconds, he has officially passed the AKC Introduction to Quarry test. Now you just have to get him out of the tunnel!

Most people don't want to dig up their yards and keep pet rats just so they can see if their terrier wants to enter an earthdog trial. The Introduction to Quarry was designed for just this purpose. Dogs need no training to participate, and the purpose is to make it a positive experience for the dog. Because this test does not lead to a title, passing or failing is not important; leaving the trial with a terrier itching to do it again is the real reward.

The basics are the same for your terrier or Dachshund, no matter what type of earthdog trial you enter: Go through a tunnel and work a rat, with a few interesting variations on the theme. The AKC offers three increasingly challenging levels of earthdog testing after the Introduction to Quarry, leading to Junior (JE), Senior (SE) and Master Earthdog (ME) titles.

In the Junior Earthdog test, the dog is released 10 feet from the tunnel entrance but the handler must remain at the release point. The dog has 30 seconds to traverse the 30-foot-long tunnel with its three 90-degree turns and reach the quarry, which he must then bark at continuously for one minute. The dog must qualify twice to earn the Junior Earthdog title. Dogs who are fast and frenzied workers have no problem earning the Junior title; however, subsequent titles that require more self-restraint can be trickier.

To earn the Senior Earthdog title the test gets considerably tougher and more like what a dog would encounter in a real hunting situation. He is released farther away and the tunnel entrance is steeper and somewhat hidden. He is also faced with a false entrance to a tunnel that leads nowhere, so he has to follow a scent trail to pick the right entrance. Once in the tunnel, he encounters two false routes that don't lead to the rat. And after he finds and barks at the quarry, the rat is blocked from view and he must respond to the handler's calls to return the way he came. Dogs who pass the Senior level test three times are crowned Senior Earthdogs.

The Master Earthdog test adds more elements that would be found in a real hunting situation. In an actual hunt a dog usually works together with another, often unfamiliar, dog, and must search over great distances for a den entrance. For the Master test, two terriers are released about 100 feet from the tunnel entrance, which is somewhat hidden and blocked with a removable obstruction. An unscented false tunnel is located along the scent line leading to the real tunnel. The dogs have one minute to locate the correct entrance, whereupon one dog is held outside while the other is allowed to enter the tunnel. Just as in a real underground den, the tunnel contains a couple of surprises: a constriction point where the tunnel narrows to only six inches wide, and an obstruction posed by a pipe the dog must push aside. The dog outside should remain reasonably quiet while the other is working; the two dogs will switch places once the first one is finished. A terrier must qualify at four trials to add the prestigious Master Earthdog title to his name.

The American Working Terrier Association also offers trials and titles, leading up the Certificate of Gameness (CG) award. Some breeds offer their own version of earthdog trials, but all basically require the dog to find and enter a hole, traverse a tunnel and bark at a caged rodent. Terrier heaven is underground.

## Earthdog Resources

AKC Earthdog Rules: www.akc.org/dic/events/perform/
earthdog.cfm

Working Terrier: www.workingterrier.com

American Working Terrier Association
N14330 County Hwy. G
Minong, WI 54859
www.dirt-dog.com/awta

Jack Russell Terrier Club of America Trials
P.O. Box 4527
Lutherville, MD 21094-4527
(410) 561-3655
www.terrier.com

## <u>LIGHT WEIGHTS AND HEAVY WEIGHTS</u>
### WEIGHT PULL COMPETITIONS

You stare with disbelief at the cart loaded with bags of dog food. You're used to looking at one bag at a time, not a half-ton's worth! But your dog is tough and strong and game. She is eager to get into harness and barks excitedly as her traces are attached to the cart holding the weight. You move her out to the end of the line to take up the slack, then move back behind the finish line and the pull begins. You call her and she throws herself into the challenge—and the cart creeps forward. With renewed effort, she gets a foothold and is now pulling slowly but strongly and steadily. She has a minute in which to pull the cart 16 feet. She never even thinks of giving up. When the cart crosses the finish line, she leaps into your arms and congratulates *you* with a face full of kisses. How can such a tough girl be so sweet?

So far she leads her weight class in weight pulled. The International Weight Pull Association (IWPA) is open to all dogs, offering six weight classes: 35 pounds and under; 36 to 60 pounds; 61 to 80 pounds; 81 to 100 pounds; 101 to 120 pounds; and 121 pounds and over.

## Weight Pull Resources

Raven's Watch Working Dog Equipment: (705) 386-2524; www.working-dog-equipment.com/dog-harness/

International Weight Pull Association: Toni Yoakam, (313) 848-8636, Mushnmom1@aol.com; Debbie Lee, (252) 357-0942, debiwpa@albemarlenet.com; www.iwpa.net

American Dog Breeders Association Pit Bull Weight Pulls: (801) 936-7513; members.aol.com/bstofshw/pull.html

UKC Weight Pulls: Michelle Morgan, (269) 343-9020; www.ukcdogs.com/weight.html

Dog Scouts Weight Pulling: (989) 389-2000; www.dogscouts.com/weightpull.shtml

St. Bernard Club of Alaska World Championship Dog Weight Pull: (907) 346-1749; www.alaskansaint.com

Working dog certificates are awarded for pulling a certain percentage of the dog's own weight. To earn the Working Dog (WD) title, your dog must pull 12 times her own weight on four occasions during the pulling season. To earn the Working Dog Excellent (WDX) she must pull 18 times her own weight four times during the season. To earn the Working Dog Superior (WDS) she must pull 21 times her own weight three times during the season.

Weight pulling originated with sled dogs and the tradition is still maintained in areas where sledding is common. While the record for a single dog pulling a cart over land is over 2,000 pounds, the record for pulling a sled over snow is over 5,000 pounds!

## On Ice
### Sled Dog Racing
It's funny sometimes how closely you can get to know your dogs just watching them from behind. Miles of watching their

## Sled Racing Resources

Blue Streak Racing: www.bluestreakracing.com

Dog Sledding News: www.dogsled.com

Iditarod: www.iditarod.com

International Sled Dog Racing Association: www.isdra.org

Mushing Dog Clubs: www.mushing.com/clubs.htm

Mushing Dog Race Schedule: www.mushing.com/events.htm

Race Schedules: www.sleddogcentral.com/schedules/
race_schedules.htm

Racing Web Sites: www.sleddogcentral.com/racelinks.htm

Yukon Quest: www.yukonquest.org

hindquarters as they stride tirelessly through the snow pulling you along behind them has put you in tune with them as you have never been with dogs before. They race along the path with the bright sunlight sparkling off the snow and lighting up the trail. The tranquil yet wild beauty of the dogs and the surroundings makes it difficult to believe you're in a race. You haven't seen another team in hours. There's a commotion up ahead . . . a checkpoint and a chance to tend the dogs and rest. Tomorrow you'll make the run to the finish. It won't matter what place you come in; crossing the finish line of a long-distance sled race is the real victory.

Long distance races like the Iditarod or Yukon Quest can be over 1,000 miles, although any race more than about 250 miles is considered long distance. Middistance races run from about 25 to 250 miles and sprint races range from a mile to 20 miles or so. A general rule is that the length of a sprint race in miles is equal to the number of dogs in the team, so a three-dog team (which is usually the smallest) would compete in a three-mile sprint, and so on. Times may be combined for two separate sprints run on consecutive days to determine an overall winner.

**Carting and Drafting Competition Resources**

Bernese Mountain Dog Club of America: www.bmdca.org

Newfoundland Club of America: www.newfdogclub.org

North American Working Bouvier Association: www.nawba.org/homepage.htm

Saint Bernard Club of America: www.saintbernardclub.org/perf_draft.htm

Most people prefer to start with sprint races, where they can spend the night in a warm bed. Winning a sprint race is exciting, but finishing a long-distance race is a personal triumph. Different dogs are better suited for different tasks, but sled dogs are never happier than when they're on the trail, no matter how many miles lie ahead of or behind them.

## DRAFTING A PLAN
### DRAFTING TRIALS

Your dog pulls the cart along the pathway. You let your mind wander back to the days when this was an everyday sight in the streets of Europe. Dogs were better suited than horses for pulling small carts along narrow crowded lanes, and were more affordable for most merchants. Eventually public outcry against the perceived "cruelty" of pulling a cart put the draft dogs out of work. Looking at the twinkle in your dog's eye and the smile on his face as he approaches the end of his mile-long pull makes you wonder how anyone could have imagined this task as inhumane. Of course, your dog will be unhitched and treated like a king in just a few minutes. After all, he'll have earned a drafting dog title.

Different breeds pull different types of draft equipment, so they may have different types of carting trials. Most tests require a wide variety of skills. The dog usually has to demonstrate he's under control by doing some basic obedience even before being hitched to a cart. This is important, because a dog pulling a cart

**Backpacking Resources**

Canine Backpackers: caninebackpackers.homestead.com/
index.html

Alaskan Malamutes: www.users.bigpond.com/amcv/backpack.
html

American Working Collie Association: www.awca.net

Chesapeake Bay Retrievers: www.geocities.com/aacbrc/bpd.htm

Samoyeds: www.samoyed.org/SCA/work.html

who is out of control can be a danger to all. Next, he has to cooperate while getting hitched up, waiting for you to get the equipment, backing into position in front of the cart and, once hitched, moving with you to a different area. While pulling the cart, he must show that he can change speed and back up. The fun part is the maneuvering course, in which he must pull the cart in curves, circles, sharp turns and out of a dead end, following the handler's voice commands. The dog may have to cross a wooden bridge. Finally, some tests have a freight haul portion over a long course in which the dog must haul loads of various weights, according to cart or sled type.

## PACK A TITLE
### *BACKPACKING AS A SPORT*

You stop to enjoy the view overlooking the valley below. Your dog stops to sniff the dirt. You give your dog some water from her pack and hike on. As much as you hate to head back to civilization, you know it's time. And you know she's almost earned her title for backpacking!

The Canine Backpackers Association offers all sorts of titles, from alpine to urban hikes and from junior to veteran dogs. Several breed clubs offer titles for backpacking. Their requirements vary according to breed. For example, an Alaskan Malamute may have to carry 30 percent of her body weight on

**Road Trial Resources**

Road Trial Magazine: www.touchmoon.com/dotters/rd-mag.html

Road Trial Rules: pages.prodigy.net/biederb/roadtrl.htm

four 16-kilometer hikes to qualify. A Chesapeake Bay Retriever may have to carry 10 percent of her body weight for five three-mile hikes.

## ON THE ROAD AGAIN

### ROAD TRIALS

It sure would have been easier to take the car. But you're on horseback and your dog is on foot. You're getting tired, but the horse and the dog appear fresh. And just a little more to go.

A Dalmatian Road Trial is one of the more unusual events available to some dog owners. It's designed to test a dog's ability to follow a horse or carriage over a distance. To earn a Coaching Certificate, a dog must demonstrate her ability to coach, which means maintaining a proper position in relation to the horse or carriage. More advanced titles of Road Dog (RD) and Road Dog Excellent (RDX) require coaching ability along with increasing endurance. For the RD, the dog has to travel 12.5 miles in three hours; for the RDX, she must travel 25 miles in six hours.

Coaching ability requires that the dog maintain hock position, which is sort of like heel position but with a horse or a carriage. Actually, with a horse it means staying within a horse length anywhere within a semi-circle behind the horse's head, as close as practicable without crowding. For a carriage, the dog can also stay just behind the horse's heels and under the carriage, as close as practicable without crowding.

# Chapter 8

# The Best Dog Toys

Some people balk when it comes to buying fancy dog toys for their dog. Of course, you're not one of them. You probably know from experience that the most expensive dogs toys are the ones your dog creates herself from your furniture, shoes and other stuff. You know that by handing your dog a toy whenever her jaws wrap around your cherished belongings, you can redirect her efforts to something more acceptable. You know that dog toys are a bargain.

The last few years have seen an explosion in exciting toy design. Never before have such stimulating toys been commercially available for dogs. You can supplement those toys with equally stimulating homemade toys.

Different dogs need different toys. Some dogs can only be trusted with the toughest toys on the market, whereas others will treasure fragile toys with utmost care. Gentle dogs can play with squeaky toys; soft latex tends to be more dog-resistant than hard plastic. Gentle dogs can also have stuffed animal toys, but be sure to remove any plastic eyes or noses. You can buy bunches of these toys at thrift stores and just bring out a few at a time.

Dogs who are tougher on their toys have fewer choices, and are restricted to larger toys made of thick rubber. Most dogs fall somewhere in between.

When evaluating the safety of any toy, consider:

- The toy should not be small enough to be inhaled or swallowed whole.
- The toy should not have parts that can be pulled off and swallowed.
- The toy should not have any sharp parts.
- Avoid linear toys such as pantyhose, strings, ribbons and rubber bands that can be swallowed; such toys can be particularly dangerous.
- Use chewable toys with caution and under supervision. If your dog can swallow a big hunk of it, it's probably not really safe. Bones and hooves are responsible for many cracked rear teeth, resulting in expensive dental bills.
- If your dog is obsessed with dissecting toys to remove the squeakers, only give him squeaky toys when you can supervise.
- Avoid children's toys stuffed with unsafe fillings, such as beans.
- Never give your dog a container in which the dog's head could become lodged. Dogs cannot pull these containers off and have suffocated when they became stuck.
- Never leave a dog unsupervised with a toy that contains a battery.

Some toys require a person on the other end. Balls, tug toys and chase toys are some examples. Don't think you can hand your dog a toy that requires a person and expect her to be entertained while you're gone. She will turn to a toy that doesn't require your presence in order to be fun, such as the arm of your sofa.

**Sources for Dog Toys**

Dog Toys: www.dogtoys.com

Dogwise: www.dogwise.com

Fido's Toys: www.fidostoys.com

Happy Dog Toys: www.happydogtoys.com

Kong Toys: www.kongcompany.com

Party Dog: www.party-dog.com

Petsmart: www.petsmart.com

SitStay: www.sitstay.com

The Puppy Shop: www.thepuppyshop.com

Today's Dog: www.todaysdog.com

There are toys available that don't require human interaction. These toys are often designed to be chewed or manipulated in order to get a food reward. If you want to use a toy as a dogsitter, be sure to provide an appropriate one.

Give your dog a variety of toys and rotate them every week so she greets them as though they were new. Include toys to chase, manipulate, chew and cuddle.

# THE TOYS

## STICK IT!
### *TOYS THAT GROW ON TREES*
What could be better than an old-fashioned stick from your own backyard? It was good enough for Lassie.

For some dogs, sticks are fine. They're easy to throw, they're easy to find and they even float. Most important, you're not out anything when you lose them.

For other dogs, sticks are not fine. Dogs who chew sticks end up with splinters in their gums and wood chips in their digestive tract. Sticks from cured lumber contain deadly chemicals. And sticks of certain lengths can poke holes in a dog's throat. That's because many dogs hold sticks by their tips and then start running around. When the other end of the stick slams into the ground, as it often does with a long stick, the end in the dog's mouth stabs the dog's throat. If you choose to play with sticks, choose short sticks with blunt ends and don't let your dog chew them.

## SOCK IT!
### SOCK TOYS
Several popular and cheap homemade toys began their lives as socks. Stuff one sock into another, knot it and you have a dazzlingly complex toy for a young puppy. Stuff a sock with crinkly paper and the toy gets even better. Put a tennis ball into the end of an athletic sock and you have a good throwing toy.

Socks as toys have big drawbacks, however. If you don't want your dog chewing up the good socks you may leave strewn about, then you shouldn't give her the idea it's OK to chew on any socks. More important is the danger if your dog eats a sock. Socks tend to be eaten in long lengths or even whole. When they pass intact into the intestines, they tend to travel along lengthwise, sometimes catching on the intestinal wall and causing it to scrunch up accordion style, even turning in on itself just like a sock. This is a life-threatening medical condition called intussusception that usually requires expensive surgery to correct. That sock toy could be the most expensive one your dog ever ate if you leave it, or other socks, laying around for him to eat while you're not looking. So sock toys are OK, but only with supervision.

## MILKING THE FUN
### MILK JUG TOYS
Take one large milk jug. Drink the milk. Rinse the jug. Throw it in the yard. No matter how hard toy manufacturers try, they'll have a hard time beating this toy for entertainment value. It makes a neat noise, it's lightweight, it can be carried and it can be

filled with treats that will leak out slowly as the dog plays. It can even be filled with water and placed in the freezer, or just filled with ice cubes, to create an icy canteen toy on a hot day.

Eventually it will get squished and lose some of its bounce. Then it's time to drink some more milk and make a new toy. Use plastic soda bottles for smaller dogs.

## BURSTING HIS BUBBLE
### SOAP BUBBLES
Soap bubbles may be the only thing remotely related to soap that won't send your dog running for cover. Just to be safe, leave off the "soap" part and simply call them "bubbles" when you talk to your dog. Nontoxic bubbles made for kids and dogs are safe and won't create a mess, even indoors (unless you spill the bottle). You can make giant bubbles, standard bubbles or zillions of bubbles. Send them flying and let your dog kill every attacking alien bubble.

## FULL OF HOT AIR
### YOUR BEAUTIFUL BALLOONS
How many times have you been told not to play ball inside? With a balloon, you can sort of play ball with your dog and maybe even do so without breaking the lamp. Inflate the balloons enough so they float easily but not so much that they pop at the slightest rough handling. Your dog will pop them eventually, so don't play with balloons if you have a nervous dog. When they do pop, clean up all the pieces so your dog can't swallow them.

## CHASING CARS
### REMOTE CONTROL TOYS
Here's just the thing for dogs who dream of chasing cars: a remote control model car! Now your dog can chase his own car around the house and when he catches it, it's the car that's more likely to get hurt.

Unfortunately, model car designers thoughtlessly designed their product for humans, so you will not be able to find a remote control squirrel or even a rawhide-flavored car. Your next best choice is a tough plastic one that can take a lot of abuse. If your dog is hesitant about chasing it, you can attach a lightweight ball to bounce behind it or even cover it with fake fur to make it more enticing.

Of course, this is just a special occasion toy. Don't leave it around to be eaten when you're not at the controls.

## In Search of the Lost Squeak
### MAKE YOUR OWN SQUEAKY TOYS

It never fails: You splurge on a deluxe squeaky toy and your dog eviscerates it in search of its voice box. Now you're left with a gutted pile of fluff.

You can help your mute toy find its voice again by replacing the squeaky. Many dog supply catalogs, as well as magic, hobby and fabric stores, carry a variety of squeakers. Even a person with sewing skills slightly better than those of a chimp can place these squeakers back inside and stitch up the toy's hide.

You can also make simple squeaky toys from scratch with a squeaker, some fabric and a bit of fluff filling. Your dog won't care that it looks more like an alien than a bunny.

## Hot Diggity Dog!
### A CANINE SANDBOX

How many times have you gazed upon the moonscape that used to be your lush lawn and cursed the crater-creating cur you unleashed upon it? Face it—dogs dig. Short of cementing over your yard, there's not a whole lot you can do about it. So you may think the idea of a digging game just can't be good. But really, it may help focus your dog's digging and keep him out of your vegetable garden.

Kids have sandboxes. Why not dogs? Most dogs like flinging sand even more than they like flinging dirt. Sand doesn't turn into mud and it's easier to brush out of most coats.

Your dog doesn't just dig for the sheer joy of digging; he digs to explore, to hunt and to occasionally find buried treasure. What if you baited his sandbox with these treasures? Wouldn't a smart dog center his mining operations around such productive lands and refrain from excavating the lawn?

You can follow instructions for making a kid's sandbox, but you should make it deeper to accommodate your dog's talent for deep excavation. Once the box has been filled with sand, take a little trowel and bury treasures at varying depths in the sand. Bury dog biscuits, big rawhide bones, balls, rope tugs, stuffed animals and squeaky toys. If you plan to leave your dog to discover these treasures while you're gone, be careful that you only bury items that are safe for unsupervised play or chewing.

Don't bury everything at once. You want to keep your dog wondering what could show up next and hoping today will be the day he hits the mother lode. The uncertainty of the game makes it more interesting, and the novelty of the finds makes them more rewarding.

A sandbox probably won't eliminate digging in the rest of your yard, but it may focus a lot of digging to that one area. And for most people, that's as good as it gets.

## CUR POOLING

### *KIDDIE POOLS*

Not since the invention of the ball has one item made such a difference in the fun content of so many dogs' lives. Kiddie pools provide a great place to cool off in summer. Throw some toys in, some of which float and some of which sink, for added fun. If your dog doesn't like water, try filling the pool with only an inch or so of water, and gradually increasing the depth as she gets used to it.

Hard plastic kiddie pools come in a range of sizes. Their only design flaw is that the plastic edge can be sharp, so if your dog has thin skin you should be careful. You can cover the edges with foam pipe insulation to make them safer. Inflatable pools come in larger sizes and don't have sharp edges. Dogs find them much more fun because they can ricochet off the sides. These pools are surprisingly tough, but they can't withstand deliberate bites.

The downside of all kiddie pools is that they must be emptied and refilled every few days, because the water begins to grow strange creatures. Fortunately, most dogs especially like the time when the hose is in the pool filling it up. The other bad part about kiddie pools is that dogs will invariably jump out of them, dig a hole just deep enough to frost themselves with dirt, and then run inside the house and jump on your bed. Lock the doggie door!

## PANDORA'S BOX
### FUN WITH PLAIN BROWN WRAPPERS

Dogs, like toddlers, have an irritating habit of preferring gift-wrapping to the actual gifts. So why not capitalize on this? Wrap a box of dog bones in newspaper and give it to your dog to rip open. Get a variety of boxes and place a special treat or toy in each. Give them to your dog, wrapped or unwrapped, and let her work to open them and get to the surprise inside.

Warning: If your dog really likes this game, keep her away from the Christmas presents!

## RACE TO THE POLE
### MAKE A POLE LURE

Not all dogs care about chasing balls. That doesn't necessarily mean they don't like to chase. Many dogs who aren't excited by thrown balls go berserk when they play with a pole lure toy. This is the same toy that young racing Greyhounds play with to introduce them to racing. Sighthounds and terriers seem to especially like playing with pole lures. It's a great way to give your dog a backyard workout, but don't overdo it.

Not surprisingly, to make a pole lure you will need a pole and a lure. The pole can be any lightweight pole about four to eight feet long. Bamboo fishing poles work well. Even better than a pole is a long horse lunging whip; it adds a springing action that makes the game much more lively. The lure can be a stuffed toy, soft rag, plastic garbage bag or piece of fur. It should be something that the dog can't get his teeth caught in or his mouth banged by. Tie the lure to the end of the pole with a sturdy string about five feet long. If you've bought a horse lunging whip it will often have a long enough piece already attached. The longer your pole and string, the faster it can go, but your string should never be longer than your pole.

Some dogs catch on right away. All you have to do is run around your yard dragging the lure and they will give chase. But most dogs, and many puppies, are more hesitant, and you may need to tease them a bit at first. Place the dog on one side of a fence and play with the lure on the opposite side, going back and forth along the fence. As interest grows, throw the lure over to his side of the fence, letting him catch it occasionally but other times popping it back before he catches it. Don't make it too easy, but don't make it impossible.

If your dog still isn't interested, try changing your lure. White plastic garbage bags are more fun than they sound. They rustle and shimmer and, in fact, they're the official lure used at sighthound field trials. The ultimate lure is created by adding a "squawker," which is a rubber contraption that makes the sound of an injured rabbit when the squawker is dragged. A dog need not have ever seen a rabbit in his life to find the sound fascinating. Squawkers, also called predator calls, are available at many hunting supply stores, as well as through the National Greyhound Association store (www.networksplus.net/nga/supply.htm).

If your dog still is not interested at this point, untie the lure, take your pole and go fishing.

For the dogs who are interested, it's time to go into the backyard with your pole lure and dog. The rest is easy. Run around the yard and let your dog chase the lure. Warning: It's easy to overdo it with this game. Be careful not to make your dog cut turns that are too sharp or take high, twisting leaps. Also be careful you don't inadvertently lure your dog into hitting a tree or other obstacle. Most of all, don't let your neighbors see you. They will be sure you've finally lost your mind.

The pole lure is good for exercising your dog in a confined space. It's great to take on trips where you don't have the chance to run your dog. You can keep your dog on a long line and still give him a quick workout.

It's also good to take on trips with dogs who aren't great about coming when called. Many people carry their pole lures everywhere because dogs who are in the middle of running away will often come running back to chase the lure—especially if a squawker is being used to alert the dog from a distance. Pole lures have probably saved many sighthound lives this way. That's why it's important not to overdo the game even if your dog is crazy about it. You always want to quit while he still wants more.

## AND THEY'RE OFF!

### A BACKYARD RACETRACK

If you have more than one dog, chances are they love to run and chase one another. And chances are one of them always wins. The loser may get so discouraged that he doesn't even want to race anymore. That's where a racetrack comes in. It lets your dogs race one another while still being separated by a fence.

Many dogs do this on their own if they're in adjoining yards. They chase one another up and down the fence until it becomes irritating—at least to you. The difference with using a racetrack is that it is only used as a special treat while the dogs are under your supervision.

Ideally, the track should be oval so the dogs can go around and around. To make a racetrack, all you need to do is put up two concentric fences. This makes an inner circle for one dog to run in and a narrower outer circle for the other dog. The outer circle should be wide enough to make the sure the dog has plenty of room to turn or run wide on the turns. The ideal surface is sand; otherwise the track can become muddy and slippery.

Some dogs don't know when to stop when they have the chance to race on their track, and you may need to rig a way to catch them if they go crazy. One way is to block the outer track in one place with a noticeable but soft barrier, such as a sheet. That will usually cause the dog to come to his senses, so you can take him off the track to rest.

## BALL AND CHAIN

### TETHERBALL

In the old days just about every yard had a tetherball set-up for the kids. Why not? It was cheap, simple and fun. Tetherball still is, and your dog will like it just as much as any kid. The only difference is that you need to hang the ball from a horizontal arm so you don't take the chance of your dog banging into the vertical pole.

One easy way to do this is to buy a circular clothesline or even a beach umbrella for your tether pole. Cover the vertical part with pipe insulation for some cushioning in case your dog hits it. Then sink a piece of sturdy pipe into the ground that's about two feet high and slightly wider than your cushioned vertical pole (it's a good idea to cushion this, too). Place your beach umbrella into the pipe, attach the tethered ball, and have fun.

You can also buy an official flexible tetherball pole. The good part about having a flexible pole is that it is safer if you or your dog runs into it. The bad part is that it's more likely to break.

Consider your dog's size when deciding how sturdy you wish to make the pole. Remember to sink the pipe a couple of feet into the ground for stability. Your tetherball court should be on a soft surface and well away from any obstacles.

You can buy official tetherballs that come with a protruding loop or a recessed bar for attaching to the tether. The loop isn't as strong and tends to hurt if it bangs into your hand or your dog's face. But, depending on your dog's jaw size, his teeth could get caught in the bar. You can also use some dog toys available at pet supply stores that come with a rope already attached. You can also place a ball or a balloon in a sack or pillow case and tie it on. Use a ball that is too large for your dog to grasp. You want her to bump it, not hang from it.

In real tetherball you would have half the court and your dog would have the other. You can use temporary fencing to divide the court in half if you're a stickler for rules. Most dogs prefer a free-form style of play in which your dog hits the ball one way and you hit it in the opposite direction, and nobody ever really gets the ball wrapped all the way around the pole. Since most dogs can hit the ball only with their nose, consider being fair and hitting it only with your head. Some dogs use their paws, in which case you can use your hands. Keep a gentle touch; don't get carried away and whack the ball into your dog.

## GET A GRIP
### SPRINGPOLE
The springpole is a great toy for tenacious dogs who like to jump, grab on to something and hang in there. It's basically a dog toy hung from a very sturdy spring. This is the ideal home entertainment system for the dog who just has to get his teeth into something.

First you need a place to hang the spring and something to hang it from. Choose an area that your dog can't get to unless you're with him. Some dogs don't know when to quit and can become exhausted or overheated unless you pull them away; this is a game that requires supervision. Find a place with a soft surface and without any objects the dog could bang into when jumping or hanging. You can hang it from a hefty tree branch, a rafter or even a strong cable strung between two trees.

The higher it's hung, the more swing it will have. That doesn't mean you should hang it off the top of your house; the more swing it has, the higher your dog can go—and the higher they go, the harder they fall. Springpoles are traditionally used for Pit Bull–type breeds, which are very tough and seem to take such falls in stride. Your dog may break under similar circumstances.

Once you've settled on a reasonable hanging spot, attach your spring. The easiest way to do this is to use a strong buckle-style dog collar and buckle it around both the hanging surface and your spring. The strongest and most reliable spring is a garage door spring. You can also use a small inner tube, such as a wheel-barrow inner tube. Using two inner tubes together will give you insurance in case one should break.

Securely attach a rope to the bottom of your spring. The rope should be long enough so your dog's hind feet can easily touch the ground and his front feet can touch the ground with a little effort when he goes to grab the lure hanging from it. Otherwise your dog will just grab the lure and hang, which provides no exercise and little fun.

Ideally, the spring should be just strong enough so your dog can pull the lure down and also place his front feet on the ground. This set-up will provide the ultimate in fun and exercise.

The lure should be something your dog can grab and hold on to tight. A real piece of cowhide, a rolled up burlap sack or some old denim jeans are all popular choices. Make sure the lure has no hard parts, such as chains or metal fasteners, that could catch in the dog's mouth or break a tooth.

Introduce your dog to the game gradually. Tease him a little and get him excited about chasing and grabbing the lure. You may need to start with it a little lower and then gradually raise it.

A few caveats:

- Springpoles have a lot in common with clotheslines. Don't expect your dog to tell the difference between denim hanging from a springpole and denim hanging from a clothesline.

- Because of their association as exercise tools used by fighting dog trainers, some people see a springpole and assume you are fighting your dogs. This is particularly true if you have a Pit Bull breed—the very breeds that enjoy springpoles the most.
- Limit play to one dog at a time to decrease the chance of injury or fighting.
- If you can't locate your springpole in a place your dog can't get to without you, loop the lure well out of reach and temptation when you're not there to supervise.

## GONE FISHING
### TUG-OF-WAR ON A FISHING LINE

Why settle for minnows when you can reel in a big one? If you have a fishing pole and a dog who likes to chase things, you can spend your afternoons fishing without leaving your backyard. Take a standard fishing pole—a surfcasting pole is ideal—and remove all the leaders and sinkers and hooks from the line. Replace them with a fake fur lure or a ball. You can cut a slit in a tennis ball so you can tie a line around it, or you can buy a ball with a fling strap from a pet supply store and use that.

You know the rest. Cast your lure and troll for dog fish.

## JUMP FOR JOY
### OBSTACLE COURSE

The sport of agility combines jumping, weaving, running, tunneling and balancing. It's a lot of fun, but the official equipment is expensive. You and your dog can have just as much fun with obstacles you make at home.

The advantage of official equipment is that it's made to hold up to lots of abuse and work with lots of different size dogs. It's also easier to whip out a credit card than it is to wield a hammer. But several obstacles are fairly simple to make and, as long as you adjust them to your dog's size, can be made so they are safe and sturdy.

The instructions here are bare-bones versions. Entire Internet discussion groups have flourished to discuss the best ways to build equipment. If you wish to eventually compete in the sport of agility, you'll probably want to make your obstacles as close to regulation as possible. In that case, check out the organizations listed in the box on page 136 for official dimensions required by the various agility organizations. You may also wish to buy pre-made equipment (see the box on page 184 for sources).

As you're building, be aware of how obstacles will look to your dog, keeping in mind that dogs are red-green color-blind. Winding a contrasting color tape around obstacles is an easy way to help them stand out from the background. Be sure to cover any sharp edges with either lots of layers of duct tape or, if possible, foam pipe insulation.

When deciding where to place your obstacles, consider that not all obstacles are safe for your dog to tackle in your absence. This is especially true if you have more than one dog. You don't want them racing around an obstacle course, pushing each other off ramps and getting into other predicaments while you're not home.

## Jumps

Jumps are simple. Depending on the size of your dog, you can turn picnic table benches or chaise lounges on their sides and have usable jumps. For higher jumps, you can use panels from large cardboard boxes, propping them up so they will fall if the dog hits them. You can place a broom handle between two cinderblocks and have a beginner's bar jump.

You can make an inexpensive bar jump using two electric fence poles as posts. Not *electrified* fence poles! Electric fence poles are lightweight posts that stick in the ground and are available at farm supply stores. They come in heights up to four feet. Pound them into the ground a little less than four feet apart. Buy a four-foot length of skinny (half-inch) PVC pipe; this will be the bar the dog jumps over. For a fancier look and more stability, slip two more four-foot pieces of half-inch PVC pipe over each upright.

You want the horizontal bar to fall off if the dog hits it, so you can't attach it to the vertical poles. Instead, clip clothespins, alligator clips or large paper binder clips around the uprights to provide a ledge on which to rest the PVC pipe. A ledge that slopes downward won't work; one with a slight lip works best.

The dog should only jump in the direction in which hitting the PVC pipe would knock it off the uprights. You can buy more horizontal bars and clips for a multi-barred jump, and you can hang a sheet from the top bar for a jump that appears to be solid but still has plenty of give.

For larger dogs, you can use larger PVC pipe, but if the upright pipes are too large you'll have to devise another way to hang the horizontal bar. Some people drill holes in the large diameter uprights and then hang the horizontal bar from pegs placed in the holes. This works, but unless the pegs are very short the bar won't fall off as easily as it should. The best solution is to use "jump cups," which are rounded cups in which the horizontal pole rests. When knocked, the pole rolls right out. Making a jump cup is a little tricky. The best way is to take a PVC end pipe and cut it into lengthwise quarters, then screw what's left of the cap part into your vertical pole.

If you don't have any land to pound posts into (maybe you got fed up long ago with your dog's digging and covered the yard with concrete), you'll have to add legs to stabilize the jump. The easiest way to do this is to add a four-way elbow fitting that enables you to place the upright section in the top of the fitting and attach one-and-a-half-foot PVC pipe "legs" to the front, back and sides. (You can also run a pipe between the two uprights to connect them at the base.) The greatest challenge here is finding the four-way fitting; if your hardware store doesn't carry them, a PVC supply company will (the agility equipment resources on page 184 will include links to these kinds of companies).

## Tire Jump

Does your dog have you jumping through hoops? Here's your chance to get back at her. The simplest hoop for your dog to jump through is a store-bought hula hoop. You can just hold it and have your dog jump through. But if you want something a little closer to an agility tire jump, you can get a tire. Depending on the size of your dog, you can use an old car tire or a tractor tire. Be sure to drill a hole in the bottom so rainwater doesn't accumulate in it.

A fancier and more lightweight solution can be made using corrugated drainpipe (it looks like a fatter version of flexible vacuum cleaner hose), which is available at any home supply store. Get about 90 inches of four-inch drainpipe and place it in the sun for awhile. As it warms it becomes more flexible, and eventually you will be able to tie it into a circle. Once you decide what size hoop you want, cut the pipe and force one end into the other. You can drill some holes and use cable ties to secure it, or if it seems to be firmly attached you can just wrap the joint with duct tape.

A cheap super-quick just-for-fun tire can be fashioned with the foam "funoodle" pool toys they sell for kids. Just bend it into a circle and tape the ends together with duct tape.

Once you've decided how high off the ground you want your tire jump, you'll need to hang it. You'll also want to secure it on both sides so it doesn't sway when the dog tries to jump through it. The ideal set-up is to secure the tire inside a square PVC pipe frame, with the vertical legs of the frame steadied by horizontal legs at the front and rear, similar to the base of the PVC jumps.

You can drill holes in the tire and attach eye loops, or you can use buckle dog collars and loop them around the tire. Use ropes, strong Velcro, or elastic bungee cords to hang and secure the tire. Leave a little give just in case the dog hits the tire. Make sure the ties going to the side can't be tripped over; you may need to put a barrier in front of them.

## Tunnels

Regulation agility tunnels are hard to beat—but they're expensive! You can make homemade tunnels simply by making arches of chicken wire and covering them with old sheets. It's good enough to have fun with!

Next best are some store-bought items. Several department stores sell a play tunnel for children. It's not as sturdy as the canine version and will be too small for large dogs, but it's good for starters. Unlike regulation tunnels, which are strong enough for a dog to bank off their sides in a curve, these tunnels will break if a dog ricochets around inside. This means they're not an ideal choice if you want to encourage your dog to power through a tunnel. Small dogs have an additional option: collapsible hoop-type containers that are often sold as laundry or gardening bags. You'll have to cut the bottom out. They're too short for the full tunnel experience, but they're good for getting the idea.

You have to keep tunnels from rolling once the dog gets in them. You can do this by driving stakes down into the ground along each side and simply nestling your tunnel between the rows of stakes. If your tunnel is strong enough you can run a bungee cord over the top from stake to stake for added stability.

## Chutes

Chutes start out just like regular tunnels, but then the tunnel turns into a collapsed fabric tube, so the dog is running blind— sort of like when he gets under the covers in your bed. Experienced dogs know there's light at the end of the chute and run right through it. Inexperienced dogs will need plenty of time and patience to learn how a chute works.

For little dogs, a plastic garbage can with the bottom removed will work fine as the tunnel entrance. For larger dogs, a plastic drum with the bottom removed works well. The drum is turned on its side, staked into place, and some nonslip surface, such as rubber matting, is glued to the inside where the dog's feet may land, for traction.

The chute part is ideally made of lightweight nylon cloth about 12 feet long. For starters, you can use a nylon-type shower curtain and just drape it over your tunnel exit. Eventually you'll want to sew the cloth into a tube so that the dog is running entirely within a tunnel of cloth, rather than having his feet touch the ground. Fancier chutes get wider nearer their exit. You may need to sew several shower curtains together or buy some fabric.

Use elastic bungee cords to secure the fabric chute to the your entrance tunnel. This works best if your trash can has a lip on it. Otherwise you may need to drill some holes and run cable ties through the shower curtain grommets, making sure no cable ties on the inside of the tunnel are anywhere your dog could get a toe snagged in them.

## Balance Beam

In agility this is called the dog walk, but it's basically the canine version of the balance beam in women's gymnastics. Of course dogs need a wider base; the object isn't to put them in danger of falling. Your choice of width will depend on your dog's size, but a 12-inch-wide board is good for most dogs.

Start low. Just place your board so it bridges two cinderblocks and you have a beginner's balance beam. Add two more boards on either end as approach and descent ramps. Your dog won't need them to hop up on a low board, but they'll be necessary later and he might as well get used to them now. Before you go farther, though, cover the surface of your boards with nonskid paint. You can do this by sprinkling a light layer of sand over wet paint.

Securing your boards becomes critical if you want to go higher than a single cinderblock; even at the low level you might as well secure them. You need to make sure the boards won't fall. And you need to do something about the gap that will appear where the angled boards meet the top board. One way to address both problems is to attach the boards together. If you're skilled with mitering edges and you never intend to move or change the heights of your boards, you can cut them to fit snugly and screw them together. A better way, that enables you to raise and lower your balance beam height, is to attach the boards together with a sturdy piano or door hinge on the underside. Use a strip of pipe insulation or a fistful of beanbags to fill the gap.

You'll also need to attach the boards to the base. Sawhorses make good bases when you're ready to go higher than cinderblocks. You can screw the boards directly into the sawhorse, or attach brackets to the sawhorse to secure the boards.

## A-Frame

If you're getting really adventurous you can add an A-frame to your obstacle course. It's usually taller but wider than the dog walk, and has no horizontal plank—the dog just goes up and then down.

The easiest way to make an A-frame is to get two old doors. Remove all the hardware and patch any holes. Use a sturdy hinge to attach them end-to-end. This should enable you to adjust the height and angle of the doors. It will also leave a gap in the top that you must fill. The best thing for this is one of those long tubes of beans used to stop drafts under doors in your house.

You will also need to prevent the doors from slipping apart when the dog is on them. This is done by attaching a chain about a quarter of the way down each door, running from door to door. The chain should be adjustable so you can change the angle of the doors, and it will have to be very long to accommodate the low angles you'll start with. Screw in some hooks to attach the chain, and then you can slip different links over the hooks to change the angle of the A-frame.

You also need to provide some footing for your dog. Start by coating the doors with paint and then sprinkling a light coating of sand over the paint while it's still wet. Then nail small slats about a foot apart width-wise across each door. You can use baseboard molding for this.

Finally, make sure the A-frame is securely fixed to the ground and that it doesn't wobble.

## Weave Poles

Weave poles are a straight line of poles set into the ground that the dog weaves in and out of. The world's easiest weave poles are simply a bunch of plungers set in a row. They have the disadvantage of being fairly easy to knock over and having a wider than optimal base, but they're great for inside practice.

An easy way to set up weave poles outside is to use a series of electric fence posts. A little fancier is a set made of fiberglass tent poles placed in the ground and then covered with thin PVC pipe. This allows the pole to flex and bend at the base when the dog hits it.

## Cavaletti

Cavaletti is a horse-training technique that teaches horses awareness of where their four feet are. It uses a series of poles placed low to the ground, sometimes at the same height and distance

## Agility Equipment Sources

Affordable Agility Equipment: www.affordableagility.com

Agility Equipment Group: www.groups.yahoo.com/group/agility-equipment/

J and J Dog Supplies: www.jandjdog.com

Pipe Dreams Agility Equipment: www.max200.com

from one another, and sometimes at varying heights and distances. The horse, or in our case, dog, is asked to calmly trot over them without knocking them down. To do so requires careful foot placement.

All you need for cavaletti is a bunch of thin PVC pipes about four feet long and four tent stakes for each pipe. Drive the first tent stake partly into the ground at a 45-degree angle. Then drive a second one next to it but angling in the opposite direction, so that they form an X shape. You can also buy pieces of X-shaped PVC. Rest the PVC pipe in the V formed at the top of the X. You can adjust the height by adjusting the angles. Repeat this, placing the pipes so that the dog can take one step between each pole.

## Buja Board

A strange piece of equipment found in many agility trainers' yards is the buja board. It's basically a piece of plywood about two feet square that rests on an underinflated or squishy ball. The ball is then placed in a little wooden frame to keep it from rolling too far. When the dog jumps on the board, the board rolls around unpredictably and the dog has a surfing experience.

## Broad Jumps

It's just as much fun to jump a broad jump as it is a high jump. But it's easier to make. Put together a quickie broad jump by placing a big piece of plywood or cardboard on some bricks. You can place four more bricks on top to keep it from flying away.

You can get a little fancier by placing boards or slats of vinyl siding on bricks, leaving gaps between them for the dog to jump over. The official AKC obedience broad jump consists of up to four angled boards separated by fairly large spaces.

## Chapter 9

# The Best Ways to Relax

You've played some games. You've gone on some outings. You've challenged your dog. She's challenged you. You've shared some adventures. Now you've both earned a rest.

Take the time to just sit in the yard with your dog by your side and watch the leaves fall and the clouds blow by. Cuddle together in front of a cozy fire on a winter's eve. Read a book while she falls asleep with her head in your lap. Brush her coat as you listen to a restful melody. Give her a hands-on home check-up. Massage her tired muscles. Not every moment has to be high activity. Relax and bond.

## RUB YOUR DOG THE RIGHT WAY

### GIVE YOUR DOG A MASSAGE

After all your hiking, jumping and playing, you and your dog may feel pretty stiff. Good luck getting your dog to massage *your* aching muscles! But you can hold up your part of the partnership by giving your dog a nice rubdown and massage. You'll find it even relaxes you. After all, several studies have shown that petting a dog lowers your blood pressure. So think of it as medicinal.

## Dog Massage Resources

Ballner, Mary Jean, *Dog Massage: A Whiskers-to-Tail Guide to Your Dog's Ultimate Petting Experience*, Griffon, 2001.

Hourdebaigt, Jean-Pierre and Seymour, Shari, *Canine Massage: A Practical Guide*, Howell Book House, 1999.

Kamen, Daniel, *The Well Adjusted Dog: Canine Chiropractic Methods You Can Do*, Brookline, 1997.

Rugaas, Turid, *On Talking Terms With Dogs: Calming Signals*, Legacy-By-Mail, 1997.

Snow, Amy, et al., *The Well-Connected Dog: A Guide to Canine Acupressure*, Tallgrass, 1999.

Tellington-Jones, Linda, *The Tellington TTouch: A Revolutionary Natural Method to Train and Care for Your Favorite Animal*, Penguin, 1995.

Whalen-Shaw, Patricia, *Canine Massage: The Workbook*, Bookmasters, 2000.

Unless you're an experienced masseuse, you should try out different massage techniques on a person or yourself so you can get verbal feedback before digging into your dog. Use different parts of your hands, such as the palms, fingertips and knuckles, along with different pressures ranging from very light to gently hard. Move your hand in different patterns, such as in large or small circles, straight lines or just move one finger at a time. Move at different speeds, from relaxing slow motion to invigorating high speed.

Then try the same moves on your dog. Find a quiet place and have your dog lie down with you sitting beside him. Start by simply placing your hand on his body. Then glide your hands one at a time down his back from his head to his tail, over and over slowly for about 15 seconds. Gently use your entire hand to squeeze the tail to its tip. You can come back to this step throughout the massage session, varying the pressure or speed of your strokes.

Next, massage his thighs using your fingers and palms in a circular motion. Move to the shoulders and upper arms and use the same movements, being sure to also include the armpits. Glide to the forechest and use your fingertips to make circling movements. Grip each leg as you did his tail and gently squeeze all the way down to his paws. Take each paw and gently squeeze it.

Gently rub up and down your dog's throat from his chin to his chest. Cup your hands around the top of his neck and make motions as though you were gently kneading dough or clay. Do this up and down his neck. You can even massage his head by gently pressing and making small circles with your fingertips on his back skull, cheeks and between the eyes. Rub his ears between your thumb and forefinger. When you're ready to stop, rest your hand on your dog for a few seconds before quietly ending the session.

If your dog is upset by any of these massage techniques, try another one or quit altogether. Watch your dog for cues that he likes what you're doing.

## PLAY DOCTOR
### GIVE YOUR DOG A CHECK-UP

You've asked your dog to do some pretty athletic things in your adventures—even if it was only running up and down the stairs a bunch of times. Now it's time to do your part as team doctor and check her for injuries or illness. Your dog can enjoy being babied and touched all over as she plays patient. You can even dress up in a nurse's uniform if it makes you happy.

Keep track of her activity level and take note if it changes. Look out for incontinence, swollen abdomen, black or bloody stool, changes in appetite, changes in water consumption or urination, difficulty breathing, lethargy, gagging or loss of balance. Weigh her once a month and keep track of whether she is losing or gaining weight.

Watching for signs of lameness. It's usually easiest to tell if she's limping at a walk or trot. Practice watching how your dog moves normally so you can spot when she moves abnormally. You may be able to see a problem more easily if you videotape her and watch the tape in slow motion. With any hurt leg, she may have a shorter stride with one front leg compared to the other; usually it's her good leg that has the shorter stride because her hurt leg will stay on the ground for just a little bit less time than her good leg will. Sometimes she will hold her hurt leg up in the air. Sometimes she may hop with it up in the air for a few steps and then put it back down. If your dog has a lame front leg her head may bob up and down more than usual when she trots.

Sometimes she will have a hard time sitting if she has sore hips. If it's her toe that is hurt, she will often stand on the rear of her foot, so her sore foot is on the ground in front of her other front or rear foot. That way she is standing on her heel of her foot and not her toe. Sometimes your dog may step with the top of her foot (instead of the bottom) touching the ground; if she doesn't fix it right away she could have a nerve injury. If she is lame she needs to rest and may need to see the veterinarian.

Feel her body all over, checking that her muscles and bones are the same on one side of her body as the other. Check for any growths, swellings, unusually colored areas of skin, sores that don't heal or any pigmented lump that begins to grow or bleed. Look out for mammary masses, changes in testicle size or discharge from the anus, vulva or penis.

Check her feet for torn or worn pads, ripped or overlong nails or toes that are misaligned or that don't match the toes on the opposite foot. Check her mouth for red, bleeding, swollen or pale gums, loose teeth, ulcers of the tongue or gums or bad breath; her eyes for discharge, cloudiness or discolored whites; her ears for foul odor, redness, discharge or crusted tips; her nose for thickened or colored discharge.

Check her gum color. It should be pink—not white, gray, blue, yellow or light with pink spots. You should able to press on her gums and have the color return within three seconds. Of course, if your dog naturally has black gums you have to check another part of her where you can see a mucous membrane.

If your dog has any suspicious signs, or if she had an accident, became overheated or nearly drowned, you should get your veterinarian's advice even if she seems OK. She may need to take some time off before embarking on her next great adventure.

## Reading Resources

### Dog Book Centers

Dog Lovers Bookshop: www.dogbooks.com

A Dog Net: www.adognet.com/store/books

DogRead: www.groups.yahoo.com/group/DogRead/

Dogwise: www.dogwise.com

Flying Dog Press: www.flyingdogpress.com

4M Dog Books: www.4mdogbooks.com

Sit Stay: www.sitstay.com

Two Dog Press: www.twodogpress.com

### Dog Magazines

AKC Gazette: www.akc.org/pubs/index.cfm

The Bark: www.thebark.com

Dog Fancy: www.animalnetwork.com/dogfancy/

Dog and Kennel: www.dogandkennel.com

Dog and Handler (Dog Sports): www.dogandhandler.com

Dogs in Canada: www.dogs-in-canada.com

Dog Watch (Cornell University): www.vet.cornell.edu/public resources/dog.htm

DogWorld: www.dogworldmag.com/dw

UKC Bloodlines: www.ukcdogs.com/bloodlines.html

Your Dog (Tufts University): www.tufts.edu/vet/publications/yourdog/

## DOG-EARED PAGES
### READ A DOG BOOK

Your dog is snoring by your side, but you're not ready for bed. It's time to play responsible dog owner and read up on dog care.

Having a dog isn't all fun. You need to train, feed and care for your dog, which means you need books on dog behavior, training, nutrition and veterinary care. Make it a point to build your doggie library and to actually read the books you own.

## You Oughta Be in Pictures
### *Scrappy's scrapbook*

You can use some of your down time to work on a photo album or scrapbook to commemorate all your adventures. You did take a camera along, right? If not, you'll just have to do everything all over again!

Working on getting good photos of your dog in action can become a rewarding challenge. Who knows, maybe you can even enter some photo contests or sell them to a magazine. Regardless, you'll have fun seeking out new places and poses. Don't forget to take a photo of your dog while he's sleeping by your side. Check out www.dogphoto.com for some inspiration.

## Be a Hero
### *Help dogs in need*

Once in awhile your dog will breathe a sigh of relief if you just let her stay home and sleep all day. Even dogs need a day off!

You have lots of time and love to share. Why not devote a portion of it to dogs in need? You can help in so many ways. Besides financial contributions, you can contribute your time and expertise. You can help groom, socialize and train shelter dogs to make them healthier and more adoptable. You can help educate school children and others in your community about responsible dog care.

You can help transport dogs to other cities or states. So-called Canine Underground Railroad (CUR) runs make use of a series of volunteers, each of whom arranges to transport a dog for a leg of his trip to a new home. Many breed rescue groups make extensive use of such runs.

You can foster a rescue dog. You can arrange a fur ball, canine carnival or meet and greet to raise money and public awareness (page 193). You can even do your part without leaving your

## Ways to Help

### *Canine Health Organizations*

AKC Canine Health Foundation: www.akcchf.org

Morris Animal Foundation: www.morrisanimalfoundation.org

### *Rescue Groups*

Breed Rescue Groups: www.netpets.com/dogs/dogresc/doggrp.html

National Breed Club Rescue: www.akc.org/breeds/rescue.cfm

house by arranging or participating in Internet auctions to raise money for worthy canine causes.

Don't forget to support veterinary research. One day you will be grateful for the advances that may save or extend your dog's life. Perhaps you will have yourself to thank.

With a dog at your side, the world is yours to explore. Take the path less followed—then get off it.

*"The greatness of a nation and its moral progress can be judged by the way its animals are treated."*
— *Mahatma Gandhi*

*Treat your dog well, treat other dogs well and treat other animals well. It's the best way to treat yourself well.*

# Index

# Q

quarantine information, international travel, 88

# R

racing
  amateur, 153–155
  backpacking, 162–163
  backyard racetrack, 173–174
  pole lure, 172–173
  road trials, 163
  safety issues, 154
  sled dog, 159–161
reading resources, 191
ready command, psychic pups, 12–13
recall relay race, 48–49
recipes, sources, 14
red light command, sit stay, 11
red rover for dogs, 56
relay races, 48–50
remembered (marked) items, retrieving, 21–22
remote control cars, toy uses, 169–170
rescue organizations, 192–193
rescue work, 122–123
resorts, doggy destinations, 80–81
retrieving
  blind objects, 22–26
  Frisbee catching, 36–37
  marked (remembered) items, 21–22
  multiple objects, 7, 21–22
  rolled ball, 53
  scent discrimination, 19–20

scent hurdles, 57–58
thrown objects, 18–19
toys, 51–52
treat-bobbing, 47–48
underwater, 20–21
rise and shine command, canine alarm clock, 10
road trial resources, 163
road trips, 74–77
rollerblading, 110
rubber toys, underwater retrieving, 20–21

# S

safety
  racing issues, 154
  toy evaluation, 166
  water hazards, 93
sailing, 86–87
sandbox, play activity, 170–171
scavenger hunt, 46–47
scent discrimination, 19–20, 57–58
scenthounds, 120–121
scenting ability
  blind retrieve, 25–26
  doggy maze, 4–5
  finding hidden objects, 54–55
  hiding the food bowl, 8–9
  scent discrimination, 19–20
  search and rescue dogs, 122–123
  target scents, 26–27
  tracking human scent trails, 27–28
  treasure hunts, 2
  treat-finding, 8